Wired Differently

The Dyslexic Scientist

Douglas B Sims, PhD

"With remarkable honesty and courage, Dr. Sims vividly captures the lived experience of dyslexia and ADHD. *Wired Differently, The Dyslexic Scientist* is an inspiring and valuable resource for clinicians, parents, and individuals seeking to understand and realize their potential."

- Nicole Ann Cavenagh, PhD, Pediatric Neurophysiologist

"This book tells an important story that goes beyond offering hope to neurodiverse students who are struggling. It should be read by teachers, university professors, academic advisors and counselors--anyone who works with students who might be experiencing the silent struggles and stigmas that come with a brain that works differently."

- Denise Tillery, PhD, Professor of English, University of Nevada Las Vegas

"There is something valuable here for every educator, from kindergarten to full professor, and for anyone navigating cognitive or neurodivergent challenges, it should be required reading. So many of us have kept our secret and our silence because we grew up being repeatedly taught the terrible consequences of not doing so – and then Sims enters the conversation and delivers what feels like a long-awaited mic drop."

- Christopher Adcock, PhD, Research Scientist, College of Southern Nevada

Printed in the United States of America.

For more information, or to book an event, contact:
douglas.sims@csn.edu

Book design by DB Sims
Cover design by DB Sims

ISBN – Paperback: 978-1-966739-11-1
ISBN – eBook: 978-1-966739-12-8

Edited by Author Bonnie Hearn Hill

First Edition: May 2026

Douglas B Sims, PhD

Table of Contents

Acknowledgments

Life is a maze of connections, interactions, joy, and at times pain that we all must navigate, and no one can do it alone.

First and foremost, I express my deepest gratitude to my wife, Karen, for her unwavering love, steadfast support, and guidance throughout our more than 35 years together. Thank you for standing beside me through every challenge, all the crazy things I did, and triumph. Without you, I would not be who I am or where I am today. Your presence has been my anchor, my inspiration, and a constant source of strength throughout my life and the writing of this book.

Together, we have raised two wonderful young adulthood, and seeing them grow and thrive has been one of the greatest joys of our lives. You have enriched our lives in countless ways and taught us perseverance, patience, and unconditional love. Watching your growth has been a continual source of pride and motivation.

To our family, thank you for your companionship, encouragement, and belief in us throughout this journey.

I extend heartfelt thanks to my friends and colleagues whose insights, conversations, and shared experiences added depth and authenticity to these pages and helped shape this work in meaningful ways.

I also acknowledge, though not with full gratitude, those who said, "You can't." Your negative and often harsh comments became fuel that kept me moving forward and strengthened my resolve to stay the course and prove success was possible.

Lastly, I acknowledge the countless individuals, especially those living with learning challenges like dyslexia and ADHD, who face obstacles every day. Your perseverance, resilience, and determination have been a constant source of inspiration. In many ways, this book reflects your strength and your journey.

Speaking Engagements & Opportunities

I am available for speaking engagements where I can share my story and encourage others, especially those who have been told their goals are out of reach. Living with dyslexia and ADHD, I was often told I would never succeed, yet through perseverance and support, I proved those doubts wrong.

My message focuses on resilience, determination, and refusing to let negativity block your path to greatness. By sharing my journey, I hope to inspire students, educators, professionals, and community members to believe in their potential and push beyond limitations.

I am happy to speak at conferences, group meetings, community gatherings, schools, universities, and other events. If you would like me to share my story and encourage others to pursue their greatness, I would truly welcome the opportunity.

Contact:
Dr. Douglas B. Sims, PhD

douglas.sims@csn.edu

Douglas B Sims, PhD

Introduction

To Every Square Peg in a Round Hole World.

Being a human whirlwind with a side of chaos might just be your superpower.

What if the things people said were wrong about you weren't wrong at all, just misunderstood? What if the struggles with dyslexia and ADHD they warned would hold you back because you were "too much" or "not enough" were actually the ingredients for an extraordinary life?

It wasn't a problem. My brain was just wired differently. In this book, I'm going to show you how those differences helped me build a career in science because sometimes success doesn't stay inside the lines.

This isn't a book about perfection. Not even close. If you're looking for neat boxes, color-coded life plans, or a five-step formula to becoming a polished corporate robot, with this is your cue to run. Fast.

This book is about breaking those boxes apart, lighting them on fire, and roasting marshmallows over what's left. It's about rewriting what success looks like, owning your story, messy, loud, brilliant, and using it to build a future no one saw coming. Including you.

I was never the kid teachers bragged about. I was the one they talked about in the teachers' lounge. You know the conversation: "Is he even paying attention?"

For the record, I was. Just not to what they thought I should be paying attention to.

I spent a long time in a system that didn't know what to do with a brain like mine. I carried labels and low expectations everywhere, like an itchy sweater I couldn't take off. I didn't just get through it. I surprised everyone, including myself. I went from struggling to read as a kid to becoming a scientist, then a professor and finally Dean of the School of Science, Engineering, and Mathematics at the College of Southern Nevada.

Yeah, that wasn't exactly predicted back in my fifth grade reading resource group.

Here's something I've learned along the way: there are still people who believe dyslexia puts a limit on what you can achieve. That it somehow caps your intelligence, your leadership, your future.

They're wrong. Completely wrong.

Dyslexia doesn't mean you're less capable, it means you think differently. Different thinking is where new ideas come from. It's where creativity lives. It's where innovation starts while everyone else is still following the same script.

A lot of the things that once felt like weaknesses, reading differently, processing information in your own way, taking the long road instead of the obvious one, those are often the very things that build resilience, creativity, and problem-solving skills.

Dyslexia doesn't hold you back. If anything, it trains you for success in ways most people never experience.

You learn to adapt.

You learn to push through.

You learn to see things other people miss.

Those skills. They matter.

If you've ever been made to feel like your dyslexia was a limitation, let me say this clearly: it's not. It's a different way of thinking. Once you learn how to use it, it becomes an advantage.

If you think those old ideas about dyslexia are gone, you're wrong.

As recently as March of 2026, a sitting U.S. president publicly questioned whether the Governor of California with dyslexia should even be allowed to lead, suggesting that a learning difference somehow makes you less capable.

Let that sink in. Not in a classroom or on a playground. At the highest level of leadership of the most powerful country in the world.

That's the kind of thinking we're still up against.

Here's the truth, dyslexia isn't a lack of intelligence, it's the brain processing language and information in unique and often creative ways. The same difference some people still misunderstand is the exact thing that helps others innovate, lead, and see the world in ways that move it forward.

This isn't just about my story; this is about rewriting a narrative that clearly still needs rewriting.

This book is part battle cry, part pep talk, and maybe a little bit of a nudge for anyone who's ever been underestimated, misunderstood, or told to "tone it down." It's about turning what makes you different into something powerful. It's also about giving yourself permission to be who you already are.

What I didn't know back then, and what I want you to know now, is this: when the world hands you a map that doesn't make sense, you don't follow it. You make your own.

If you're a student drowning in doubt, a professional tired of pretending to be "normal," or someone who's been told to "be realistic" one too many times, consider this your permission slip.

Stop apologizing, stop shrinking, and for the love of caffeine, stop trying to be someone else.

There's no pity party here. This is the start of something bigger, a shift in how we see ourselves. Neurodiversity isn't a flaw, it's just a different kind of brilliance, so stop trying to fit in and start standing out.

This is what it looks like to build success on your own terms. You are not broken. You're built differently. Honestly, the world should probably get ready for that.

Chapter 1

The Label That Never Fit

In October 2023, I found myself standing beneath the soft glow of a chandelier in a grand ballroom at the University of Nevada, Las Vegas, waiting for my name to be called for 2023 Alumni of the year for the College of Science. I was one of several honorees that evening. As the emcee's voice echoed through the room, and I stepped toward the podium, everything slowed down like a movie scene, except I didn't have a dramatic soundtrack or wind blowing through my hair (missed opportunity, honestly). The applause, the lights, the faces all melted into a muffled blur. And then it hit me: this wasn't just an award. This was a shiny, hard-earned "you didn't completely screw it up" trophy. A golden punctuation mark at the end of a sentence I've been writing for as long as I can remember, built not on ease or perfection, but on hard-earned lessons, stumbles that left marks, recoveries I never saw coming, and a determination powered mostly by coffee and sheer will.

They told me I was broken. Lazy. Unteachable. But I wasn't the problem. My wiring was just different, and somehow, against every expectation, I turned that difference into winning. Standing under that chandelier, I realized something: the people who change the world aren't the ones who stay inside the lines. They're the ones who redraw them.

As I took the stage, something unexpected happened. My thoughts didn't drift to recent achievements, fancy job titles, or academic milestones. No. My mind time-traveled back to those dimly lit elementary school classrooms, where my proudest daily achievement was ducking humiliation faster than a kid ducks broccoli.

I remember the fluorescent lights buzzing overhead in my fourth-grade classroom, the cheap, waxy scent of Crayola markers in the air, and the scratchy texture of the construction paper on my desk. We were all working on these big, colorful posters for a history assignment, "Famous People of the Wild West." I had chosen a sheriff, thinking it sounded cool. Brave. Important. A protector of people.

I carefully drew the figure with his badge, cowboy hat, and dusty boots. But when it came time to write the word "sheriff" at the top, I got stuck. I spelled it "Sherrif." I wasn't sure, but I hoped it looked close enough.

When it was my turn to hold up my poster, I walked nervously to the front of the class. My heart is beating 100 miles per hour. I turned it around, showing off the drawing. I was actually kind of proud of my poster. But before I could say a word, my teacher squinted, tilted her head, and said loudly, "You spelled sheriff wrong. That's not even close." She further asked me, "Didn't you think to check it before bringing that up here?"

The classroom went dead silent for a beat. Then it erupted in laughter.

She continued, shaking her head in front of everyone. "Honestly, sometimes I wonder if you're just not trying hard enough. This is fourth grade, not kindergarten."

And just like that, something cracked inside me.

The laughter stuck. For weeks, maybe months, "stupid" followed me down the hallway, whispered behind me at recess, etched in pencil on the edge of my desk when the teacher wasn't looking. I stopped raising my hand. Stopped trying to stand out. I tried to blend in, shrinking into myself like a small animal hiding from a predator. I'd lower my eyes and make myself invisible, curling up metaphorically in my seat, hoping the spotlight would move on.

But it didn't. That moment had already been stitched into the fabric of who I was becoming; a quiet shame I carried, even when the laughter faded.

Those classrooms were my battlegrounds, where I fought invisible wars, against letters that refused to stay still, against a body that wouldn't stop fidgeting, against the shame of being "different," and against teachers who mistook my struggle for laziness and my differences for failure.

Standing there, facing a crowd now applauding in approval for me receiving the UNLV 2023 Alumni of the year for science, I couldn't help but marvel at the irony.

Sometimes life has a funny way of lining up its plot twists, recognition, awards, and applause before reminding you where the story really began.

Okay, now back to how this story came to be.

My Colleague, the Dean of the College of Science at UNLV, and the man who nominated me, had seen what many hadn't seen, the labor of love behind the work I did at the College of Southern Nevada. He recognized the student-centered programs, the long hours, the tireless advocacy. He didn't know the whole story, the setbacks, the fight against dyslexia and ADHD, or what it feels like to have your brain work differently than everyone else's. He only saw what it turned into, the strengths, the results.

But when the UNLV Dean said he nominated me for this award, it hit me. It was personal. It meant I wasn't just pushing through anymore. I was finally seen.

That's why this award meant so much. It wasn't just about institutional recognition. It was a symbolic middle finger to every teacher, professor, and peer who wrote me off. It was a moment where the kid who couldn't read a sentence without stumbling now stood center stage, being honored for helping thousands of students find their voices.

Even as I stand here, my past never fully leaves me. Those echoes still whisper, but they no longer control the volume. I've learned to tune them out when it matters most. Because they didn't define me anymore. They sharpened me. Strengthened me. They gave me the tools I needed to reshape my world.

This wasn't just a celebration of success. It was a reclamation of identity. A public declaration that I had never been broken, I was simply misread, misunderstood by a system that didn't know where to place someone like me, misjudged by people who saw the struggle but not the strength it forged. What I went through didn't knock me down; it helped me learn how to hold my ground.

This award belongs to every kid who'd ever sat in the back of a classroom, heart pounding, praying they wouldn't be called on to read aloud. It belongs to every adult still haunted by red pen corrections and the quiet shame of being "slow," "unfocused," or "not living up to potential." It's for those still in the trenches, still questioning their worth, still pushing forward even when the world kept stacking the odds.

I tell my story to pull back the curtain. To expose what it's really like to live with dyslexia and ADHD in a world built on neat rows and rigid expectations. Because the truth is, the struggle was never just about learning differently. It was about surviving in a system that was never built to see us. To share the weight of constantly feeling like you're a few beats off, out of sync with the tempo everyone else seems to follow. But then one day, you stop trying to match their rhythm. You realize that your beat, your pace, your way of thinking are not broken. They are a gift.

Living with learning differences demands constant recalibration. It's a lifestyle. It demands humor when you want to scream. It requires resourcefulness in moments when the tools just aren't there. Above all, it calls for relentless determination, the kind that doesn't make headlines but shapes lives.

Yes, modern tools and technology have opened doors, we've made progress in awareness, however, let's not pretend the path is smooth. It's still steep, isolating, and confusing.

That's why it matters so much that we speak out and that we keep speaking out. Every story we tell becomes a bridge for someone, somewhere, waiting for that bridge.

As I looked out from the podium that night, something deep clicked into place. This recognition wasn't the end of anything, it was a powerful mile marker on a much longer, winding road. The real victory was every tiny step that led there.

That 2023 Alumni award sits quietly on a shelf. A polished, physical reminder of what's possible when you refuse to give up. But when the darkness creeps in, and it still does, I don't look at the trophy. I look at who I've become. And I remind myself of the truth: I've already walked through fire. I've already proved them wrong. I've built something lasting and real.

Before I got here, before I embraced any part of myself, I had to learn how to survive a system that was never built for someone like me.

Chapter 2

Invisible Struggles, Unseen Strengths

As I stood there with the award in hand, what most people didn't realize was how many invisible battles had been fought to reach that moment. That applause wasn't just for what I had done, it echoed for every moment I had almost given up. To understand the victory, you have to understand the war.

When I was growing up, dyslexia and ADHD weren't just misunderstood; they were practically mythical creatures. If anyone mentioned them at all, it was usually in hushed tones, as if discussing a top-secret condition or an embarrassing rash. More often, they just slapped on labels like "unmotivated," or my personal favorite: "not living up to his potential." A phrase that's somehow both vague and incredibly insulting; 10/10 would not be recommended.

Certainly, the world has made some progress, yay, awareness! But the road is still riddled with potholes of misinformation, outdated stereotypes, and the kind of casual dismissals that make you want to throw a textbook across the room. Ironically, I probably couldn't read that textbook anyway.

For me, dyslexia and ADHD weren't just academic speedbumps. They were full-blown road closures with detours through self-doubt and imposter syndrome. They didn't clock out when the school bell rang. They followed me everywhere: into friendships, into my marriage, into every big dream I dared to have. They were like that clingy friend who just won't take a hint.

Once, I interrupted a friend mid-conversation (talking about a romantic breakup), to explain how a box fan worked. Not because it was relevant, just because my brain decided it was time for an impromptu TED Talk on airflow dynamics. One minute she was crying about how "he never really listened," and the next, I'm passionately describing how the fan's motor uses electromagnetic induction to spin the blades. I even made a swooshing sound effect. Because, obviously, that helped.

She wasn't consoled. Weird.

Here's the twist: ADHD and dyslexia didn't just shape my struggles. They also shaped my drive. They taught me to work harder, dig deeper, and find back doors when the front was locked tight. When the world expected me to fail, succeeding became the ultimate plot twist for me.

I wrote this book because I know what it feels like to sit in a classroom, heart pounding, eyes locked on a page that refuses to make sense. I know what it's like to hear your name called, not for praise, but to be made an example of. I know the quiet humiliation of being left behind, and the loud resilience it takes to keep showing up anyway.

From the start, I didn't fit the mold. I colored outside the lines, sometimes literally, sometimes metaphorically, and I was quickly labeled for it. Teachers assumed I didn't care. Classmates didn't understand why I was "weird." I learned early on that if I didn't advocate for myself, no one else would. The message was clear; people like me weren't meant to succeed.

I never accepted that message, not deep down.

My journey has been a blend of setbacks and breakthroughs. I've hit walls, stumbled, gotten back up, and sometimes run headfirst into another wall just for good measure. Dyslexia was a constant frustration, words jumbled, comprehension delayed, reading aloud a nightmare. ADHD brought its own chaos: a brain that revved like a sports car with no brakes. I acted before thinking. I took risks that blew up in my face. I got in my own way more times than I can count.

But every mistake taught me something. Every misstep became part of a much larger lesson plan, one not taught in any school. ADHD gave me energy, passion, and a creative fire that's hard to contain. Dyslexia forced me to think differently, solve problems with unconventional strategies, and connect dots others couldn't see. Over time, I realized that what had once made me feel broken was actually the source of my strength.

It didn't happen in a vacuum. I had help along the way, mentors who saw promise when others only saw problems. Above all, I had my wife. Her belief in me, especially during the moments when I didn't believe in myself, became the foundation I could always return to. She didn't just see my potential, but she also reminded me of it, daily, until I started to believe it myself.

The Fried Shrimp Incident

There's a story my wife and I still laugh about now, but at the time? Let's just say it was not a highlight in my journey to academic greatness.

We were both students at the time, and the plan was simple, meet at my apartment, head to campus, and rendezvous at the student union before class. A normal couple's weekday routine.

We left, each in our own car, waved, smiled, and drove off.

Except I didn't go to school.

I turned my car in the opposite direction, rolled into Long John Silver's like it was my destiny, ordered a tray of fried shrimp and fries, then drove back to my apartment, parked it on the couch, and fired up The Original Star Trek like I was boldly going nowhere with my life.

Meanwhile, she was sitting in the student union. Waiting. Probably wondering if I got hit by a bus, abducted by aliens, or just forgot what day it was. Since there were no cellphones back then, she was left to wonder as she sat in class. Meanwhile, I was eating hushpuppies and watching Captain Kirk have another inter-species relationship.

Yep. I did that.

As you can imagine, she was not thrilled. But what matters more than the shrimp (though it was good), or the episode (a classic), is why I did it.

The truth is, I was drowning.

That moment summed up exactly how I felt about myself back then, lost, numb, and exhausted. I didn't belong at that university. I was convinced of it. The lectures, the textbooks, the endless expectations all felt like noise I wasn't built to process. I wasn't incapable. I was defeated. I couldn't see a future beyond the next hour. Even thinking about the next day felt like standing at the base of Mount Everest with flip-flops and a juice box.

In that darkness, the voices of the past came roaring back. Every teacher who made me feel stupid. Every red-inked test. Every time I was told to "try harder" when I was already trying as hard as I could. Those voices screamed.

There were days when the weight of it all got so heavy that even existing felt like too much. There were thoughts I'm not proud of, days when I truly questioned whether the world would be better off without me in it. That's where I was, alone, ashamed, sitting in a dingy apartment with fried shrimp and Star Trek because reality felt too heavy to carry.

But my wife (then girlfriend) never gave up on me.

She could've walked. She could've said, "You clearly don't want this." But she didn't. She didn't shame me. She didn't lecture me. She saw the despair I was trying to hide, and she stayed.

Looking back, that was the first time I realized love doesn't always show up with grand gestures. It shows up with fried-shrimp patience and a seat at the student union for someone who didn't deserve it yet.

After my second academic suspension, she both comforted and fought for me. She was patient, yes, but also persistent. She knew there was more in me than the world had yet seen. Slowly, she began to help me find it.

She taught me how to study, how to write, how to process information in a way that worked for my brain, the stuff no one ever taught me in school. She filled in the gaps left behind by an educational system that was never designed for students like me.

She wasn't just my cheerleader; she became my teacher. She showed me how to break things down, one paragraph at a time, one reference at a time. She helped me create schedules when my ADHD brain refused to acknowledge the existence of clocks. She helped me learn how to swim in academic waters I had been drowning in.

And that, dear reader, was my turning point.

It didn't happen overnight. But from that point on, I started stacking up small victories. A passing quiz. A decent paper. A conversation with a professor that didn't end in frustration or failure. I was the king of grade C.

And those small wins started to add up, one after another until I realized I had strung together a life full of momentum. A life that, yes, still had failures, but also had purpose. A life built on both success and survival. On grit. On a second chance I almost threw away if not for my wife.

So yes, there was a day I bailed on college for fried shrimp and Star Trek, but there was also a day I chose to try again—because someone believed in me before I believed in myself. And she still does.

She's what saved me. Her faith. Her time. Her stubborn, quiet refusal to let me disappear. And yeah, she still keeps an eye on me anytime we pass a Long John Silver's, just in case.

The truth is, there are millions of people like me, children sitting in classrooms right now, trying their best and being told it's not good enough. Adults in workplaces where their brilliance goes unnoticed because it doesn't fit a traditional mold. To them, I say this: your story is still being written, and it is far from over.

My road hasn't been a smooth, upward trajectory. It's been more like a roller coaster designed by someone with a dark sense of humor, complete with surprise drops, sideways loops, and the occasional "Did I just lose a shoe?" moment. But I've kept moving forward. That's what matters. Not how fast. Not how gracefully. Definitely not without screaming. Just forward.

This book is a reflection on that wild ride. It's about what's possible when we stop trying to fit into someone else's mold, when we embrace the way we're wired, even if that wiring sometimes feels like it was installed by a sleep-deprived electrician, and when we dare to challenge the world's narrow, outdated definitions of intelligence and success. It's a love letter to resilience, a standing ovation for neurodiversity, and a friendly reminder that thriving doesn't have just one look. Sometimes, it shows up with mismatched socks and a stubborn refusal to quit

I'm writing this for anyone who's ever been underestimated, misjudged, or misunderstood. For every person still trying to find their place in a world that doesn't always feel like it was made for them. Whether you have dyslexia, ADHD, or some other "difference," know this: your mind is not broken. Your story is powerful. Your perspective is needed.

The traits that once made me feel out of place are the same ones that now help me innovate, connect, and lead. They didn't disqualify me from success. They rerouted me. They gave me a unique voice, one I now use to lift others up.

If you're still running life's race and wondering whether you'll ever win, know that you can. It won't always be easy. In fact, it almost never is. But every struggle brings you closer to the person you were meant to become.

Dyslexia and ADHD are lenses, ways of seeing the world differently. And sometimes, seeing the world differently is exactly what the world needs.

Before we dive deeper into the rest of this story, I want to provide a little context, about what dyslexia and ADHD really are, how they affect people like me, and why understanding them is essential to understanding not just my life, but the lives of so many others still waiting to be seen, heard, and believed.

Because the truth is, I didn't beat the odds. I just refused to stop trying.

Living with Dyslexia: Challenges and Insights

While I'm not a psychologist, I'll do my best to explain what dyslexia and ADHD are, and how they affect people like me.

Dyslexia affects one in five people, making it one of the most common neurodevelopmental disorders. It accounts for 80–90% of all individuals diagnosed with learning disorders (Shaywitz, 2003).

For me, it looked like this: sitting in front of a five-sentence paragraph for thirty minutes, rereading the same line over and over, praying my brain would finally catch up.

This condition impacts a person's ability to read, write, and spell, despite having average or above-average intelligence. Research also points to a strong genetic component such as 1 in 3 children born to a parent with dyslexia will inherit the condition, highlighting its familial nature (American Psychiatric Association, 2013).

And dyslexia rarely travels alone. About 30% of individuals with dyslexia are also diagnosed with Attention Deficit Hyperactivity Disorder (ADHD), a condition that disrupts focus, impulse control, and organization. The overlap of the two can make everything from reading to simply sitting still feel like running a mental marathon in flip-flops.

This is why early diagnosis and intervention are so important—because when these conditions go undetected, they don't just affect academic success. They shape self-worth.

Dyslexia is a language-based condition and, therefore, affects reading, writing, and language processing. It is one of the most common learning differences, yet it remains widely misunderstood. Dyslexia is not a reflection of low intelligence, laziness, or lack of effort. Instead, it is a specific learning difference rooted in how the brain processes language, particularly the decoding and recognition of written words (Lyon et al., 2003; Shaywitz, 2003). Dyslexia can vary significantly in its severity and impact, with some individuals experiencing mild difficulties and others facing profound challenges that affect multiple areas of learning and daily life (Pennington, 2009).

Common characteristics of dyslexia include difficulty decoding words, challenges with spelling and writing, slow and laborious reading, and problems with phonological awareness, such as linking sounds to letters or breaking words into syllables (Snowling & Hulme, 2021). Individuals with dyslexia often excel in oral comprehension but struggle with reading comprehension, as their difficulties with decoding text hinder their ability to focus on the meaning (Wolf & Bowers, 1999).

Additionally, individuals may experience problems with sequencing, short-term memory, and organizing written information, which can extend into other areas like math and time management (Stanovich, 1988; Vellutino et al., 2004).

Dyslexia is typically diagnosed through a comprehensive evaluation process. This includes cognitive tests that assess verbal reasoning, memory, and phonological processing skills; reading assessments to measure reading accuracy, fluency, and comprehension; and a review of family history. Diagnostic evaluations are commonly conducted by clinical psychologists, or speech-language pathologists trained in identifying learning disorders. Early diagnosis is critical, as it enables the implementation of targeted interventions and strategies that can significantly improve learning outcomes and self-confidence (Fletcher et al., 2007).

Intervention strategies for dyslexia often focus on structured literacy programs, which emphasize phonics-based instruction to improve decoding and spelling skills (Torgesen, 2002). Assistive technologies, such as text-to-speech software and audiobooks, are also invaluable tools that help individuals access content and reduce frustration associated with reading (Snowling & Hulme, 2021). Accommodations like extended time on tests, access to oral instructions, and note-taking support can level the playing field in academic and workplace settings (Vellutino et al., 2004). Under the Individuals with Disabilities Education Act (IDEA), public schools are legally required to provide appropriate assistive technologies and accommodations to students with documented learning disabilities to ensure they receive a free and appropriate public education (FAPE) in the least restrictive environment (IDEA, 2004).

Despite its challenges, dyslexia is often associated with unique strengths, such as creativity, out-of-the-box thinking, and strong problem-solving abilities (Eide & Eide, 2011). Many individuals with dyslexia excel in fields that require spatial reasoning, storytelling, or artistic expression, showcasing how their differences can become strengths when properly understood and supported (Wolf & Bowers, 1999). By fostering environments that celebrate neurodiversity and leveraging the talents of those with dyslexia, society can unlock the potential of individuals who think and learn differently (Stanovich, 1988).

As awareness of dyslexia grows, so too does the recognition of the importance of early diagnosis, tailored interventions, and ongoing support. By reframing how we view dyslexia, from a deficit to a difference, we can empower individuals to overcome challenges and thrive in ways that enrich us.

Living with ADHD: Impulsivity and Ingenuity

ADHD, or Attention-Deficit/Hyperactivity Disorder, is a complex neurodevelopmental disorder characterized by persistent patterns of inattention, hyperactivity, and impulsivity that interfere with daily functioning and development (Barkley, 2020; Faraone et al., 2015). While it is often diagnosed in childhood, ADHD affects individuals across the lifespan, with symptoms evolving as they age (Nigg, 2017). It is not a one-size-fits-all condition; its manifestation can vary significantly across genders, cultural contexts, and developmental stages (Hinshaw & Scheffler, 2014). Women and girls with ADHD, for example, are often underdiagnosed because their symptoms are more likely to present as inattentiveness rather than hyperactivity, leading to their struggles being overlooked, misattributed, and minimized (Quinn & Madhoo, 2014).

ADHD is categorized into three types:

- **Inattentive Type**: Individuals with this type often have difficulty sustaining focus, organizing tasks, and following through on instructions. They may appear forgetful, easily distracted, or prone to daydreaming (Willcutt, 2012).
- **Hyperactive-Impulsive Type**: This type is characterized by physical restlessness, excessive talking, and impulsive actions such as interrupting conversations or making decisions without considering consequences (Biederman & Faraone, 2005).
- **Combined Type**: The most common presentation, this type features a mix of inattentive and hyperactive-impulsive

symptoms, creating challenges across multiple areas of life (American Psychiatric Association, 2013).

Spoiler alert: I'm Combined Type, through and through.

I've made decisions faster than most people can find their car keys. Bought things I didn't need, started projects I forgot halfway through, and said "yes" to ideas before anyone even finished explaining them. Hyperactive? Check. Inattentive? Also check. Basically, I'm a human version of a browser with 47 tabs open, and one of them is playing music, but I can't figure out which.

But here's the twist: all that chaos? It's also my magic. My impulsivity has launched businesses, sparked wild ideas (some that actually worked), and pushed me into opportunities most people would overthink until the moment passed. So yeah, I'm Combined Type, and while it can be a liability, as with dyslexia ADHD has also been a superpower.

Of course, it's not all wins. There was a time I drafted a seventy-page proposal for work overnight, drank eight cans of Diet Coke, and forgot to attach the entire proposal to the email before hitting send. That's ADHD: 100% effort, 0% attention to detail. My brain is so often flooded with thoughts and ideas that get me excited. I can feel like a rock star. But the implementation of these ideas looks more like a raccoon stuck in a trash can.

Accurate diagnosis is a sophisticated process. Behavioral assessments are typically completed by teachers, parents, and individuals themselves, to get insight into how symptoms affect individuals at school, work, and home (Pelham et al., 2005). Clinical evaluations are conducted by trained professionals, such as psychologists, psychiatrists, or pediatricians, who use established diagnostic criteria, such as those outlined in the *Diagnostic and Statistical Manual of Mental Disorders*, Fifth Edition (DSM-5-TR) (American Psychiatric Association, 2013).

To ensure accuracy, the diagnostic process includes a careful rule-out procedure. Professionals assess whether symptoms might be better explained by other conditions, such as anxiety disorders, depression, or learning disabilities, which can sometimes mimic or coexist with ADHD. This comprehensive approach is crucial for providing an accurate diagnosis and determining appropriate interventions (Barkley, 2020; Pliszka, 2007).

ADHD management typically involves a combination of strategies tailored to the individual's needs, including behavioral therapies, organizational skill training, educational accommodations and medication such as stimulants or non-stimulants (Wilens & Spencer, 2010). Support systems, including family involvement and workplace adjustments, also play a critical role in helping individuals with ADHD thrive (Faraone et al., 2015).

While ADHD presents significant challenges, it is also associated with unique strengths. Many individuals with ADHD demonstrate creativity, high energy, and an ability to think unconventional, which can lead to success in innovative and fast-paced environments (Hallowell & Ratey, 2011). Recognizing and leveraging these strengths, while addressing the challenges, is key to supporting those with ADHD across all stages of life (Nigg, 2017).

Misconceptions About Dyslexia and ADHD

One of the most pervasive misconceptions about dyslexia, often linked to ADHD due to overlapping challenges in attention and learning, is the idea that it is simply a matter of reversing letters or numbers. In the 1980s, this misunderstanding became widespread, and dyslexia was inaccurately reduced to a visual processing issue (Torgesen, 2002; Snowling & Hulme, 2021). People imagined that those with dyslexia, like me, saw words and numbers in a jumbled or backward fashion. To this day, I am frequently asked if this is what I experience when I read or write.

In third grade, I once wrote the word horse as "hors", and the teacher asked if I was making up a new language. I wasn't. It just looked right to me. Welcome to the magical land of dyslexia, where the letters play musical chairs and still expect you to get an A.

This reductionist view does a disservice to the complexity of dyslexia. Dyslexia is not primarily a visual problem; rather, it is a language-based learning disorder that affects the ability to decode words, spell, and read fluently. For individuals like me, the experience is not one of seeing backward letters but of grappling with the brain's difficulty in connecting written symbols to their corresponding sounds. Reading is slow and labor-intensive, and writing often involves additional effort to ensure accuracy and coherence.

ADHD is also misunderstood. Many people incorrectly assume that ADHD is just a lack of focus or hyperactivity, overlooking the nuanced ways it affects executive function, emotional regulation, and task persistence. Both ADHD and dyslexia illustrate the need for better public understanding of neurodevelopmental disorders to reduce stigma and promote effective support strategies.

The persistence of these misconceptions highlights the importance of education. By fostering a more accurate understanding of conditions like ADHD and dyslexia, we can shift the focus away from outdated stereotypes and toward actionable approaches that support those who live with these challenges.

How Dyslexia and ADHD Affect Individuals

Dyslexia and Attention Deficit Hyperactivity Disorder (ADHD) profoundly impact not just academic and professional lives but also personal relationships. The misunderstandings by the general public surrounding these conditions often lead to feelings of isolation and shame, as societal judgments, criticism, and disparaging remarks reinforce the belief that individuals with these challenges are somehow "less than." These misconceptions do more than create barriers; they erode trust and connection in relationships at every stage of life, from childhood friendships to adult partnerships and professional collaborations.

When I was young, the ridicule and judgment were relentless. Struggling to read aloud in class or failing to keep pace with traditional learning methods drew scorn from classmates and, sometimes, teachers who dismissed my challenges as laziness or lack of effort. These experiences didn't just affect my academic confidence; they fractured my ability to connect with others. The fear of being judged or humiliated led me to withdraw from social interactions, further deepening my sense of isolation. The impulsive and hyperactive nature of ADHD often compounds this problem. Impulsivity is frequently misinterpreted as rudeness or carelessness, leading to misunderstandings and strained relationships with peers and authority figures.

Unfortunately, this cycle of shame and retreat isn't confined to childhood. It extends into adulthood, manifesting in personal, professional, and academic settings. In higher education, where understanding and inclusion should thrive, the stigma persists. I've heard colleagues entrusted to guide and inspire students, make remarks that are not only disheartening but outright harmful. Statements like "Students registered with the Disability Resource Center (DRC) when at University will never graduate and should consider dropping out" betray the fundamental mission of education. These words validate the fears of students with dyslexia or ADHD, reinforcing the idea that they don't belong, which can devastate their confidence and self-worth.

This bias extends far beyond the classroom. Not long ago, I found myself among a group of public-school teachers. One of them, a teacher who works with students facing challenges like mine, casually remarked, "I work with students who have an individualized education plan (IEPs); you know, the dummies in school." I was stunned and deeply offended. Her comment didn't just reflect her own ignorance; it perpetuated a damaging stereotype that students with learning differences are inherently less capable.

Unable to let it pass, I told her, "I had an IEP in school and now have a PhD in a field of earth sciences." My response was a statement for every student who has ever been written off because of their learning differences.

For me, these attitudes are a painful reminder of how deeply misunderstandings about dyslexia and ADHD are entrenched in our society. Relationships with colleagues, mentors, and even friends often became fraught because my challenges were misinterpreted as incompetence or disinterest. In professional settings, tasks requiring strong reading, writing, or organizational skills exposed me to the same judgments I faced in school. Colleagues often assumed my struggles were due to lack of effort rather than a genuine difference in how I processed information. Over the years, my hyperactivity and impulsivity, core traits of ADHD, have often been mistaken for unprofessionalism, leading to strained workplace dynamics and a sense of alienation.

These misunderstandings damage relationships that could otherwise provide support, collaboration, and mutual growth. Impulsive behaviors, difficulty focusing, or struggles with reading and writing are often seen as character flaws rather than differences in cognition. This lack of awareness can lead to frustration, resentment, and even estrangement in personal and professional relationships.

Breaking this cycle of judgment and misunderstanding demands systemic and cultural change. Institutions, from schools to workplaces, must recognize the profound impact of dismissive attitudes and discriminatory comments. Teachers, professors, and employers need training not just to understand the challenges associated with dyslexia and ADHD but to value the unique strengths and perspectives of those who live with them. For example, higher education faculty must reflect on the immense harm caused by prejudiced remarks, like suggesting that students with disabilities are incapable of success. These beliefs are not only untrue but actively undermine the potential of individuals who may already feel marginalized.

Fostering empathy and awareness is crucial to creating inclusive environments. People must understand that dyslexia and ADHD do not make someone "deficient." Instead, they represent different ways of processing information and solving problems, ways that often lead to extraordinary creativity and innovation when properly supported. Celebrating achievements, providing accommodations, and emphasizing strengths can transform relationships and create a culture where neurodiversity is respected and embraced.

For me, the journey has been one of the uphill battles, not just against the challenges of dyslexia and ADHD but also against the biases and judgments of others. If it weren't for my resilience, the belief of a few key mentors, and the unwavering support of my wife, I might have internalized the negative messages and given up. I often think of the many individuals who may not have the same support system, who hear disparaging remarks and begin to believe they don't belong. The ripple effects of these misconceptions can be devastating to individual confidence and also to relationships with those who could offer encouragement, collaboration, or connection.

To create real change, we must dismantle the stigma surrounding dyslexia and ADHD and replace it with understanding, respect, and celebration of differences. This shift is not just about improving outcomes for individuals, but about enriching our relationships and society by unlocking the potential of everyone, regardless of how they think or learn. Dyslexia and ADHD may present challenges, but they also offer unique lenses through which to view the world, perspectives that can deepen relationships, foster creativity, and drive meaningful change.

Education, family, workplaces, and personal relationships should not be battlegrounds of judgment and exclusion. While it shouldn't be a battleground, people are people and are always trying to one-up the person next to them, especially the person with the weakest self-confidence in the room. They are almost always the most judgmental toward others. Instead, these environments should be spaces of empathy, growth, and mutual support. By shifting societal attitudes, we can build environments where individuals with dyslexia and ADHD are not only understood but embraced for their contributions, allowing relationships to thrive in ways that are deeper and more authentic.

Perceptions in Educational Settings (Flawed Educational Approach to Neurodiversity)

In both public and private schools, students with dyslexia or ADHD are often labeled as "problematic" or "unmotivated," reflecting a widespread misunderstanding of their unique challenges and needs. Teachers, frequently overburdened with large class sizes, limited resources, and inadequate funding, are often under-trained in recognizing and addressing learning differences. This lack of understanding and other contributing factors can unintentionally exacerbate the difficulties faced by these students, creating an environment where they are more likely to fall behind academically and socially (Fuchs & Fuchs, 2006; Shaywitz, 2003; Snowling & Hulme, 2021).

Misunderstanding and stigma frequently result in punitive disciplinary actions rather than supportive interventions. For example, a student with ADHD who struggles to sit still or follow instructions may be reprimanded for being "disruptive" rather than provided with strategies (i.e., opportunities for movement) to manage their symptoms. Similarly, students with dyslexia may be labeled as "slow learners" because they require more time to read or write, without consideration of their intelligence or creative potential. These negative perceptions often lead to exclusion from advanced academic tracks, limiting opportunities for these students to fully engage with their education (Barkley, 2020). Moreover, the lack of tailored teaching strategies, such as multisensory learning techniques or alternative assessment methods, often results in frustration, poor performance, and a growing sense of inadequacy in students with learning differences (Vellutino et al., 2004).

The challenges do not end in K-12 education. While individualized education plans (IEPs) exist in K-12 settings to provide tailored support under the Individuals with Disabilities Education Act (IDEA), higher education relies on Disability Resource Centers (DRCs) to fulfill a similar role. However, the DRC system in colleges and universities often lacks the authority or enforcement power to ensure that accommodations are consistently implemented. Unlike K-12 systems, where IDEA regulations carry legal weight, higher education institutions operate under the Americans with Disabilities Act (ADA) and Section 504 of the Rehabilitation Act, which mandate equal access but are less prescriptive about how accommodations are delivered (Madaus & Shaw, 2006).

In practice, this often leaves students with learning differences at the mercy of individual professors. Some faculty members, shielded by their claim of tenure, academic freedom, or administrative reluctance to intervene, refuse to fully comply with accommodation requirements. Some view accommodations as optional or unfair for other students, dismissing the need for extended test times, alternative assignments, or other supports as "special treatment." Others just lack the training or empathy to understand how critical these accommodations are to level the playing field. The result is a patchwork of compliance where students must advocate for themselves repeatedly, often with little recourse if their requests are ignored (Newman et al., 2011).

Unfortunately, administrators often lack the "teeth" to enforce compliance. Even when students report non-compliance to the DRC, the system of DRC staff, Administrators', and Deans' feel powerless to force a professor to follow the rules. This leaves students feeling unsupported and alienated, forced to navigate a system that places the burden of enforcement on them rather than the institution. For students with dyslexia or ADHD, who already face significant challenges in academic environments, this additional obstacle can be overwhelming, leading to frustration, disengagement, and, in many cases, dropping out to never return (Stanovich, 1988).

The perception that students must conform to a rigid mold, be it square, round, or rectangular, reinforces the cycle of exclusion. Those who don't fit are often left to fend for themselves in an environment that rewards conformity over creativity and innovation. This is especially troubling in higher education, where some of the most educated and intelligent people in the world are tasked with preparing the next generation of scientists, social scientists, educators, and leaders. When these institutions fail to fully engage and support all students, they lose out on the contributions of individuals who think and process differently, missing opportunities for groundbreaking ideas and diverse perspectives.

Addressing these systemic issues requires more than surface-level compliance. Higher education institutions must prioritize training for faculty on how to support students with learning differences, emphasizing that accommodations are not privileges but necessary tools for achieving equity. Administrators need to take a stronger stance, ensuring that professors follow accommodation requirements regardless of tenure or academic freedom, and creating accountability mechanisms to enforce these standards (Fletcher et al., 2007).

Moreover, fostering a culture of inclusion means recognizing that neurodivergent students bring unique strengths to the table, creativity, resilience, and problem-solving skills that enrich the academic community. Institutions must go beyond merely tolerating these differences to actively celebrating and leveraging them through initiatives such as offering flexible learning options, establishing mentorship programs, expanding disability resources, and encouraging ongoing professional development focused on neurodiversity.

Ultimately, shifting perceptions in educational settings is about valuing all students and ensuring that every individual can succeed, regardless of how they learn or think. By addressing the gaps in enforcement, training, and culture, higher education can move closer to fulfilling its promise of fostering innovation, diversity, and excellence for all learners.

Past and Present Perceptions

Historically, individuals with dyslexia and ADHD were often dismissed as "slow learners," "daydreamers" (my personal favorite), or "troublemakers," with little to no acknowledgment of their unique neurological profiles (Barkley, 2020; Shaywitz, 2003). Educational systems, lacking the tools and understanding to support such students, frequently funneled them into remedial programs that were poorly equipped to meet their actual needs (Fletcher et al., 2007). These students were stigmatized. Their struggles were misinterpreted as laziness or moral failure instead of being recognized as signs of a different way of thinking (Stanovich, 1988).

I still remember what my ninth-grade Earth Science teacher told my mom during a parent-teacher conference; "He's not up to par and he'll be lucky to graduate high school."

That moment stuck with me, not because I believed it, but because so many others did. Then, there was my ninth-grade math teacher. She pulled me aside one day, looked me straight in the eye, and said, "You think differently, and that's good."

I still remember what shirt I was wearing. That one sentence, from one person, gave me more fuel than any curriculum ever could. Of course, that glimmer of hope didn't last long. Just a few weeks later, my 9th grade social science teacher brought me crashing back down to Earth with another lovely prediction:

"You're not going to graduate from high school, Doug."

This emotional ping-pong became the backdrop of my education.

Teachers and parents, often operating within rigid and under-resourced systems, emphasized conformity over individuality, not out of malice, but because it was what the system expected of them. Unfortunately, this well-meaning compliance sends the wrong message: that the student is the problem, not the system itself (Vellutino et al., 2004).

Even when parents, like mine, try to push back against this system, things don't always get better. Their efforts are often met with resistance rather than resolution. Teachers, already overwhelmed, often interpret parental concern as criticism, and that tension can trickle down to the student.

That's exactly what happened to me. My mother became concerned when I struggled to read and came home from school exhausted, frustrated, and defeated. She asked for testing, accommodations, anything that might help. Instead of partnership, she faced defensiveness. One teacher even told her, "Maybe he just doesn't try hard enough."

The result? I became the "problem kid." Her advocacy, though fueled by love, unintentionally painted a target on my back. I could feel the change in the teachers' tone, the way they marked my homework a little more harshly, the sighs when I asked a question. One teacher even told me, within earshot of others, "If your mom spent more time helping you at home instead of blaming us, maybe you wouldn't be so far behind."

I never had the heart to tell my mom how much worse things got. Instead of opening doors, her efforts closed them. Instead of support, I got silence. Instead of collaboration, I was met with resentment. Her advocacy, noble as it was, deepened my isolation.

This dynamic followed me for years. From kindergarten through graduate school, I was either overlooked, underestimated, or dismissed. I was constantly reminded, both directly and indirectly, that I didn't fit. If you don't fit, you're easy to ignore. That message seeps into your bones.

Long before I embraced my differences as strengths, I had to first survive them. I developed tools that helped me survive in classrooms that weren't designed for someone like me. But for all their usefulness, they were just that: survival tools. They didn't erase the quiet sting of shame, the years of being misunderstood, or the labels that had etched themselves into my identity.

I could organize my notes, but I couldn't organize the pain. I carried the weight of every eye-roll, every insult, and every time a teacher made me feel small. Those scars, mostly invisible, would come roaring back when I least expected them.

All that pain became fuel to stand out, to break the mold, and to fight for something better.

Even in the worst environments, there were always a few people; mentors, professors, or peers who saw something different in me. Who looked past the labels and helped me see the possibility within the chaos. They helped me uncover what I now call my "hidden strengths."

Their encouragement gave me permission to rewrite the story the world had handed me.

To them, I am profoundly grateful. These were the people who didn't need a diagnosis to recognize a student worth investing in. They didn't change the whole system, but they changed my trajectory. Sometimes, it only takes one person believing in you to cancel out a thousand who don't.

Thankfully, things are changing.

In recent decades, perceptions of dyslexia and ADHD have started to shift. A growing body of research now highlights the strengths often associated with these conditions: creativity, problem-solving, innovation, and grit (Eide & Eide, 2011). As a society, we're finally starting to move away from "disorder" toward "difference." Assistive technologies, from text-to-speech software to AI learning aids, have opened doors that were once locked tight (Faraone et al., 2015).

We now have high-profile trailblazers, like Richard Branson, Steven Spielberg, and Barbara Corcoran, who openly credit their success to the very conditions others once saw as liabilities. Their stories prove something that so many of us need to hear, being wired differently doesn't make you broken. It makes you innovative. It makes you valuable.

Advocacy groups, researchers, and countless brave individuals have fought to raise awareness and dismantle outdated stereotypes. Slowly, society is beginning to understand that there is no single way to learn, to succeed, or to demonstrate intelligence. That understanding is building a more inclusive world, one school, one workplace, one conversation at a time.

We still have a long way to go. But we're moving. And for the first time, we're not walking that road alone.

I'm not walking it ashamed anymore. I'm walking it proud, and with purpose.

Chapter 3

Discovering my Dyslexia

Childhood is often remembered in soft hues of laughter, innocence, scraped knees, and afternoon naps. But for me, childhood didn't come in soft tones. It came in sharp edges and loud colors, fast-moving scenes, and an ever-present undercurrent of confusion. I was a whirlwind of curiosity and energy, a kid who couldn't sit still even when I tried. I loved learning, but my brain had a way of moving faster than my body, faster than the lesson, faster than the world around me.

From a very young age, I knew I was different. I could feel it. I wasn't like the other kids who sat quietly in their chairs, feet flat on the floor, eyes gliding across the page like they'd been trained by monks. I fidgeted, bounced, tapped my feet like I was auditioning for a one-kid percussion band. My hands were always in motion, if there had been a fidget toy Olympics, I would've taken gold. My thoughts? Less of a train and more of a stampede. They came in hot, fast, and completely out of order, like a flock of caffeinated pigeons fighting over breadcrumbs.

And still, one question haunted me even more than my inability to sit still for more than thirty seconds: Why did words, the very building blocks of learning, feel like a jumbled mess of spaghetti letters no one taught me how to untangle?

Looking back now, people call my story "inspirational." (Thanks, I guess) But living it? It was frustrating, demoralizing, and about as fun as a pop quiz on a Monday morning when you forgot your pencil and your will to live. It was filled with small, cutting failures that reinforced what teachers had been telling me for years. Being called on to read out loud felt like being handed a live grenade with a "Good luck!" sticker. I'd stumble over simple words, the letters swimming like they were training for the backstroke, and then came the dreaded sighs, the giggles, or worse, the stares of pity.

Each time, a little piece of me folded inward, hiding behind sarcasm, fake confidence, or my go-to defense mechanism: humor. Because if you can't read the paragraph, you might as well try to get a laugh, right?

Teachers labeled me distracted or a difficult student. Classmates saw me as "the weird kid" who couldn't keep up. Slowly but surely, I started to believe them. That sense of being broken, of being "less than," stuck to me like a sticker I couldn't peel off, no matter how hard I tried.

That ache, that relentless pressure to prove myself, to finally be "enough," to live up to expectations I was never built for? It wore me down. It still does if I'm being honest. It's also what brought me here. That blend of struggle and survival. Shame and sheer stubbornness. It's why I'm writing this, because I've lived the questions. Maybe, just maybe, you're living them too

As a child, I didn't have the words to explain what ADHD or dyslexia meant. All I knew was that my experience of the world didn't match anyone else's. People liked to toss around simplified definitions. "Oh, he sees letters backwards." or "He can't sit still." It was so much more complex than that.

My brain worked on an entirely different operating system. It wasn't just letters that didn't make sense. It was language itself, how it was processed, stored, retrieved. Reading, writing, spelling, even math, they all came through garbled. As if my mind was constantly translating a foreign language no one else had to learn. The wiring was different. And I felt that difference every single day.

Dyslexia was like trying to learn from a radio station playing a different song than the one everyone else was dancing to. And ADHD?

It dialed everything up, curiosity, emotion, distraction. My thoughts would ricochet from one idea to another in milliseconds. I was unfocused because I cared about everything all at once. My brain didn't filter; it just absorbed.

Put those two forces together, and life felt like a constant obstacle course. Everyone else had a map. I was making it up as I went, tripping, re-routing, trying not to fall too far behind. I felt like I was running a race with my shoelaces tied together.

Even today, my ADHD hasn't gone anywhere. It still lives with me like an over-caffeinated coworker who doesn't know when to stop brainstorming. My mind is a 24/7 idea machine, spitting out everything from brilliant insights to bizarre hypotheticals like, "Could squirrels run their own podcast?" And writing this book? It's chaos. Beautiful, frustrating chaos. ADHD keeps me inspired, but it also tosses my thoughts in the air like a game of mental Jenga. Still, I've learned to embrace it. This is just how my brain throws a party.

Yet, in the middle of all that noise, there was something else quietly forming, something I couldn't see back then. A strength. A stubborn resilience. A perspective that would one day become my greatest asset.

Those years of feeling different, of being othered, shaped me. They taught me to pay attention to the edges, to question assumptions, to think sideways when everyone else went straight ahead. I didn't know it at the time, but those same challenges that made me feel broken were building something inside me. A capacity for empathy. For creativity. For persistence.

The isolation of those early years was real. I felt different, I felt alone. Words were battles. Attention was fleeting. Frustration was constant. Every day felt like a test I hadn't studied for, a performance I wasn't ready to give. Beneath the performance was fear. Fear of being exposed. Of failing publicly. Of never figuring it out.

Somewhere in the mess, in the fidgeting and the struggle and the misread words, there was a spark. And that spark, hidden under layers of doubt, would eventually catch fire.

That's the story I'm telling now. Not one of perfect success or easy answers, but of hard-won progress. Of embracing a brain that refuses to follow instructions. Of turning what once felt like curses into tools for connection, for impact, for purpose.

This chapter is the beginning of that journey. The truth of what it was like to grow up wired differently. The hurt, the humor, the heartbreak, and the hope.

Struggling with Reading, Writing, and Math

In kindergarten, while other kids were busy discovering the magic of reading, eyes wide, fingers tracing each word like it was a treasure map, I was staring at letters that clearly had a personal vendetta against me. They flipped, reversed, and danced across the page like unruly performers in a chaotic off-Broadway production called "Nope, Not Today." And when my ADHD wasn't steering my attention out the window, across the room, or into a vivid world where I was a dinosaur astronaut saving kittens from space pirates, I was locked in an invisible cage match with the alphabet. Spoiler: the alphabet was winning.

In subsequent grades, reading aloud in class became a recurring nightmare, like a horror movie where the villain was silent until the teacher called your name. I'd watch my classmates take their turn, words flowing from their mouths like they were born reading bedtime stories to themselves in the womb. Then it would be my turn. The book would tremble in my hands like it knew what was coming. As I tried to decode the words, I could feel every pair of eyes boring into me like heat lasers. My mouth would stumble, trip, freeze. I wasn't just reading; I was being exposed. Publicly. In high definition.

One afternoon in fourth grade, I got stuck on a single word, "through." It looked like the easiest word on the page to everyone else, but to me it might as well have been written by an alien. I tried sounding it out over and over, like maybe if I stared at it long enough it would feel bad for me and turn into a different word. My voice kept getting quieter each time, like it was slowly giving up too. A couple kids in the back started giggling, not super loud, but loud enough that it felt like surround sound in my head. The teacher corrected me and told me to keep going, but at that point the letters on the page started swimming around like they were doing laps in a pool. My face felt so hot I was pretty sure I could fry an egg on my forehead. I kept wishing the bell would ring, or that the fire alarm would magically go off, or honestly that a meteor would hit the school just to save me. When the class finally moved on, I slid down in my chair and pretended to read along, but inside I had already made up my mind about something, reading wasn't just hard, it was embarrassing. If my school life really was a horror movie, that was definitely the jump scare scene, the one where everyone else laughs but you are still screaming inside.

Writing wasn't any easier. My attempts to form letters looked less like English and more like a series of ancient symbols last seen on a crumbling cave wall. Spelling tests were pure torture, a weekly reminder that my brain was running a completely different operating system, probably one last updated in 1987.

Teachers tried to help. Some offered gentle encouragement, bless them. Others, not so gentle. "You just need to try harder," they'd say, with the motivational tone of someone suggesting I jog to the moon. Trying didn't magically rewire my brain. It didn't make the letters stop breakdancing on the page. It didn't make things click the way they seemed to for everyone else. Instead, it made me tired, frustrated, and quietly convinced I was broken.

I remember my fifth-grade teacher handing me a thick packet of reading homework one Friday like she was passing out Halloween candy, except this was the opposite of a treat. She told me if I read each passage three times, it would get easier, like repetition was some kind of cheat code for my brain. So that night, I sat at the kitchen table staring at the first paragraph while everyone else in the house moved on with their evening. I read the same sentence over and over until the words started looking fake, like someone had made them up just to mess with me. By the third time through, I wasn't really reading anymore, I was guessing and hoping the sentence would somehow make sense on its own. When I finally finished, I felt exhausted, like I had run ten laps in my brain without moving an inch. The next Monday, when she asked if it was easier, I nodded even though it wasn't, because explaining that it still felt impossible somehow felt harder than the homework itself. Moments like that didn't make me stronger, they made me feel like no matter how hard

I tried, something inside me just wasn't working the way it was supposed to.

I wasn't, but it took me a long time, and a lot of internal pep talks, to believe that.

One of my earliest memories, one that still sits sharp and heavy, is from first grade. I was supposed to be practicing letters in my composition book, a routine assignment for most of the class. For me, it felt like being asked to push a boulder uphill. The letters wouldn't come out right. My hand wouldn't cooperate. I lagged behind, struggling to finish even a single line. While the rest of the class stood at the door, lined up for recess, I sat alone, tears streaking down my cheeks, my pencil gripped like it might help me win the war.

The teacher didn't make it easier. She called me "stupid," "dumb," right there in front of everyone. Then she looked straight at me and said, "Doug, you are holding up your class, and if you keep this up, they're not going to want to be your friend." Her voice carried through the classroom and settled inside me, becoming a voice I'd hear for years to come. You think that made it easier to make friends? Not a chance. When you're publicly humiliated for something, you don't understand and can't control, it's like being painted with a target. Kids notice. They remember.

I learned quickly that if I wanted to survive, I had to hide it. I had to mask my struggles, bury the frustration, pretend I was fine. I started to develop what I now know is a common trait among kids with learning differences, the ability to fake it. To smile when I was lost. To laugh off mistakes. To fly under the radar. It didn't solve anything, but it spared me from being singled out. Over time, the problem didn't seem to be with the words or the books. It felt like the problem was me. "Why can't I get this?" I'd whisper to myself in quiet moments, tears building when no one was around. I wanted to succeed. I wanted to learn. But the door in my brain felt locked, and no matter how many times I turned the key, it wouldn't budge.

At home, my parents tried. My mom read to me every night. She sat with me, practiced letters, encouraged me. Her love was unwavering, but even she couldn't break through whatever was happening in my mind. Progress came painfully slow, if at all. Every failure deepened my fear that I just wasn't cut out for this world of learning that everyone else seemed to understand so naturally.

My dad, like so many fathers of the 1970s and 80s, was the provider. He worked long hours and came home for dinner or to catch a game. He loved me, that much I never questioned, but he didn't quite know how to talk about what I was going through. My learning issues made him uncomfortable. Not because he didn't care, but because he didn't know how to help. He didn't talk about them. Instead, he showed his love in the ways he knew how: steadiness, routine, and reliability. He was the anchor, even if he couldn't steer the ship.

As I got older, I became better at hiding, like, Olympic-level hiding. I learned when to keep my head down, when to smile and nod like I totally understood what was going on, and when to let the spotlight pass me by like an overly enthusiastic substitute teacher with flashcards. I built a mask, one that said, "I'm fine," even when inside I felt like I was duct-taping everything together with anxiety and hope.

And it worked, sort of. It helped me dodge the worst of the ridicule, the sighs, the eye rolls. It also left me feeling like I was walking this road alone. Like I was the only one secretly struggling, the only one fighting this invisible battle, and slowly, quietly, losing.

That mask may have helped me survive the classroom, but it came with a price. It silenced me. It taught me to be ashamed of who I was, and it buried a part of me that desperately wanted to be seen. Back then, I didn't know what dyslexia was. I didn't understand ADHD. I only knew that the world felt too fast, too loud, too demanding, and that I couldn't seem to keep up. All I wanted was to be normal.

I didn't yet know that the very things that made learning so hard would later become the roots of my resilience, and that the pain of being different would one day become my purpose. I was still deep in the struggle, still trying to survive a system that wasn't built for kids like me.

Even then, something in me refused to give up.

Red Flags or Just Quirks? Early Years of 'Huh?

In the early years of my education, the term "learning disabilities" was tossed around like a catch-all net for kids like me, kids who confused teachers, defied neat little boxes, and made lesson plans spontaneously combust. Back then, it didn't feel like a diagnosis so much as a shrug. "We don't know what's wrong with him, so let's just call it this and move on." It was a label so vague it was practically whimsical, if you weren't the one wearing it like an itchy sweater with your name embroidered on the back.

The truth is, nobody really understood what I was dealing with, not the teachers, not the system, not even me. Instead of support, I got judgment. Instead of curiosity, I got condemnation. Teachers labeled me "unmotivated" as if it were a diagnosis of its own. Honestly, they weren't completely wrong. I was distracted, but I wasn't trying to be. Did they really expect a 6-year-old not to wonder how many pencils he could stick into the ceiling tiles during math time? That's just basic physics and childhood wonder.

Some teachers quietly dismissed me as a lost cause. Others went full oracle. "He'll never graduate," they'd say, with the smug certainty of someone making a bet at the racetrack. They got stuck on repeat in my head for years. They planted seeds of doubt, shame, and somewhere underneath it all, an annoyingly persistent seed of defiance.

I started to question everything. Reading, writing, spelling, math, basically anything taught in a room with fluorescent lights and worksheets felt like climbing a mountain in roller skates. But give me a broken toaster or a pile of scrap metal, and suddenly I was MacGyver. I remember thinking, okay, maybe I can't spell "definitely," but I can definitely rewire this lamp. Priorities, right?

One parent-teacher conference is seared into my memory like a bad tattoo. My mom, who was often the only adult who hadn't given up on me, sat across from my teacher, who looked like she'd aged five years just from having me in her class. No sugarcoating. "He's just not applying himself," the teacher said, like I was a defective glue stick. "He's not up to par. I recommend holding him back a grade or two." I watched my mom's face fall, and I remember sitting there thinking, fantastic. I'm already flunking at first-grade life.

Some teachers turned my struggles into public performances. They'd call me out in front of the entire class as if they were in charge of an educational roast. "Why can't you sit still? Trying to distract everyone else, or is this just for my benefit?" Naturally, this gave the kids all the ammunition they needed. I became "the dumb kid." The one who could not spell. The one who couldn't sit still. The one who couldn't finish a worksheet without getting up five times. I developed the reflexes of a ninja, dodging spitballs, insults, and the occasional flying eraser.

The bullying wasn't even imaginative. Just a steady diet of "stupid," "idiot," and "dummy." Frankly, their lack of creativity insulted me as much as their words. Meanwhile, my ADHD ensured that even when I wanted to focus, I couldn't. The smallest sound, the tiniest movement, the glint of light on a pencil, any of it could derail my attention completely. I couldn't even get a good comeback in before my thoughts ran off in another direction.

Key point here: School felt like a battlefield, and I was going in unarmed.

What stung most was the adults who should've known better. The teachers. The ones who were supposed to help me. I remember one in particular who told me, "You'll never amount to anything," right before handing me an assignment to color-code the states on a U.S. map. Imagine being told you're a failure and then being asked to stay inside the lines. If I had a dollar for every time I was told I'd never succeed, I probably could've skipped school altogether and started my own spite-fueled hedge fund.

The truth is that school was terrifying. I dreaded walking through those doors every day, because I knew I was stepping into a space where I didn't belong. Not really. I was hyper, distracted, and behind in reading. I stuck out like a neon sign in a dark room, and not in a way that earned sympathy. The only thing I became truly skilled at was avoiding attention, which is tragically ironic when you're the loudest, most energetic kid in the room without trying.

Looking back now, the absurdity of it all makes me laugh. Almost. Because buried in all that shame and chaos was a kid trying his damnedest to make sense of a world that didn't make room for him. A kid who was being written off by people who couldn't see that the very traits they criticized, curiosity, energy, imagination, were the same ones that would one day become his greatest strengths.

In those early years, I didn't know that. I just knew I was losing a game I didn't even know how to play.

Wait, I'm What? Shocking Diagnosis Reveal

The summer between sixth and seventh grade was supposed to be a break from school, a time to reset, ride bikes, and forget that fractions existed. For me, it turned into something else entirely. My mom, exhausted and heartbroken from watching me struggle year after year, decided it was time to get answers. So off we went to a child psychologist.

I didn't fully understand what was happening, I just knew I was about to spend a perfectly good summer day indoors, taking a series of tests that felt part game, part interrogation, and 100% confusing. One minute I was stacking blocks, the next I was answering riddles, and somewhere in there I was asked to repeat strings of numbers like I was being trained for a secret code-breaking mission.

What came next changed everything, and yet, in that moment, explained almost nothing. A few fancy words were scribbled on a report, some diagnoses handed out, and suddenly, I wasn't just the kid who couldn't sit still or spell "necessary." I was officially different. Certified, labeled, and sent back into the world with a folder full of paperwork and a brain still buzzing with questions.

Dyslexia. ADHD.

Those were the words the psychologist handed us, wrapped in clinical certainty, as if finally putting a name to the storm would calm it. Finally, there was a label for why I couldn't seem to keep up. A label for why reading felt like decoding a secret language and why my thoughts never stayed in one place for long. But if anyone expected those words to bring clarity or relief, they didn't understand the reality of what it meant to be different in a world that values sameness.

The decision to seek that diagnosis came after one of the most demeaning years of my life. My sixth-grade teacher, someone who was supposed to guide and encourage, not bring me down, said I wasn't "up to par." She said these things out loud. In front of the class. Often. She was cruel. Her mission, it seemed, was to make me believe I couldn't succeed. She even demanded that I be held back a grade. She said it to my mother like it was the most logical solution in the world.

Thank God my mom refused to accept that fate for me. She stood her ground, challenged the teacher, and won that battle, but the damage had already been done.

Sure, I now had my labels, dyslexia, hyperactivity, the usual suspects. I also had something else, a memory that was, and still is, nearly photographic. I can remember scenes from when I was barely 2 years old, like someone installed a DVR in my brain with unlimited storage. Every stumble, every failure, every win, every moment of shame or pride, they're still in there. Crystal clear. While most people forget what they had for lunch yesterday, I can replay the sound of my teacher's voice as she called me "stupid" with absolute accuracy.

It's a strange paradox. I wrestled with reading, but once I read something, once I managed to absorb it, it was locked in for life. Focus was always a challenge, but forgetting is not in my wheelhouse. My brain has always felt like a tornado on the outside and a filing cabinet on the inside. Those tests simply confirmed what I already knew: my brain worked differently. It just took me a while to figure out that different wasn't a defect. In fact, it was the source of something powerful.

At that time, the diagnosis felt like a spotlight. Another way to be singled out and to feel isolated. I didn't suddenly understand myself better. I just had a new reason to feel like I didn't belong. The psychologist explained: "He's NOT lazy or incapable. His brain processes information differently. He's intelligent. He just learns in a way that doesn't match the system."

That explanation clicked for my mom. I, however, was still a sixth grader trying to make sense of a world that kept telling me I was wrong for being the way I was.

To her credit, my mom didn't waste time. She threw herself into action like a woman on a mission. That summer, she found a reading specialist. Every Saturday, for the next three years, I gave up cartoons and sleep-ins to sit in a small room with a woman who, for the first time in my academic life, didn't treat me like a broken machine.

She didn't rush me. Didn't talk down to me. She broke reading into steps, into systems, into patterns I could finally understand. We sounded out words, practiced rhythm, built fluency brick by brick. Progress was slow. Sometimes it felt invisible. But it was there. And for the first time, I felt like someone believed in me, not the version of me I was pretending to be, but the real one. The one who'd been hiding under layers of defense for years.

No matter how much I was improving, I knew one thing for sure: if I wanted to survive socially, I had to keep hiding.

The trauma of my sixth-grade teacher's public ridicule had left a permanent imprint. I became hyper-aware of how others saw me, of how every mistake might be interpreted as a lack of intelligence rather than a different way of thinking. I became a master of disguise. I masked. I memorized everything I could, avoided reading out loud, guessed when I didn't know. I kept a running checklist in my head of how to avoid being found out.

That skill, masking, is one I honed with precision. It wasn't about deception. It was about protection. I wasn't trying to fool anyone. I was trying to hold onto what little confidence I had left. I didn't want pity or attention. I wanted peace. And so, I buried the signs of my struggle as deep as I could.

As I grew older, I started to realize I wasn't the only one doing this. So many students with learning differences walk through their school days performing. They don't show their struggles. They survive them, quietly, but at a high cost. That constant need to fly under the radar, and avoid judgment, is exhausting. Over time, it chips away at you. You start to believe that your value depends on how well you can hide.

Even now, more than four decades later, I still remember the techniques my tutor taught me. Her voice still echoes in my head when I get stuck: Break it down. Sound it out. One piece at a time. She didn't just teach me how to read; she gave me tools to face a world that often feels as if it's written in a language I wasn't meant to understand.

The habits I picked up in those early years, the ones built around survival, left their mark too. I became a master of blending in, of laughing things off, of quietly burying the struggle under a layer of "I'm fine." I learned, not in any classroom but through lived experience, that being different was something to hide. That struggle meant weakness. That asking for help was basically sending out an RSVP to embarrassment. It took me years, decades, honestly, to unlearn all of that.

Eventually, I realized that my dyslexia and ADHD aren't burdens, they're built-in features, not bugs. They're not glitches in the system; they ARE my operating system. They've shaped how I think, how I solve problems, how I approach everything from spreadsheets to half-baked midnight ideas that sometimes turn into actual success. They've fueled my drive. They've forced me to look at things sideways, upside down, and inside out, which, as it turns out, is exactly what innovation looks like.

That reading specialist changed my life. Not because she "fixed" me, but because she saw me. Really saw me. At a time when I was barely holding it together, she offered patience and hope. And sometimes, that's all a kid needs.

To anyone out there hiding their neurodivergence, I see you. I was you. I know what it's like to live with the weight of trying to appear "normal." There is nothing weak or shameful about being different. There's power in understanding yourself. In accepting the parts of your brain that others may not understand.

Dyslexia and ADHD don't go away. You don't outgrow them, but you can grow with them. You can stop running from them, stop hiding behind the masks. Because the truth is, your value doesn't come from how well you blend in. It comes from how bravely you stand out.

And sometimes, the very things that once made you feel broken are the things that will set you free.

The Impact on My Family and Me

When I was diagnosed with dyslexia and ADHD, the weight of those words didn't fall only on me. They landed squarely on my parents' shoulders too. For them, it was a strange cocktail of relief and fear. Relief that there was finally a name, an explanation, a reason why school had been such a battleground for me. But also fear, deep, nagging fear. Would I always struggle like this? Would I be able to succeed in school, or would this be a lifelong sentence of being "behind"?

For me, the diagnosis was both a turning point and a burden. It gave me an answer to the question that had haunted me for years: Why can't I read like the other kids? And the answer wasn't "Because you're stupid." It was, "Because your brain processes information differently." That truth didn't suddenly make reading easier. It didn't remove the struggle. But it gave the struggle a context, and that changed everything.

My mom didn't waste time with grief or denial. She dove headfirst into research like a mother preparing for a PhD in advocacy. She read everything she could find on dyslexia, books, journals, reports. She didn't just want to understand it; she wanted to know how to fight it. She became my fiercest protector, my translator in a world that didn't speak my language, and my champion when the system seemed determined to leave me behind.

I didn't grow up in one of those picture-perfect families. We were real people living a real life in the 1980s. There were bills to pay, jobs to hold, and stress that lived quietly in the corners of our home. My parents didn't have bottomless resources. They weren't wealthy. They were just two hardworking people trying to give their kids a fighting chance in a world that didn't come with an instruction manual.

One of the most important decisions my mom made was to find a reading specialist tutor who could help me build the skills I desperately needed. But this wasn't some convenient, down-the-street solution. No. She scraped together the money for reading support, because tutors like that weren't (and still aren't) covered by insurance, and drove me across the Las Vegas Valley for a one-hour session every Saturday. And when I say, "across Las Vegas," I mean the kind of drive that required coffee, gas, and patience.

I didn't realize it at the time, but those Saturdays were an act of love. While other kids were lounging in pajamas watching cartoons, I was in a small room, facing words that didn't want to make sense. While I groaned and dragged my feet at first, deep down, I knew I needed it. I just didn't have the words for that kind of gratitude yet.

That belief didn't shield me from everything. While my mom was working tirelessly to help me catch up, her efforts unintentionally made things harder for me at school. She wasn't afraid to push teachers or question school policies. She spoke up when I was ignored or mistreated. She fought for me like any mother would, and as I've already shown earlier in this book, some teachers didn't appreciate that. Her advocacy became a trigger for their resentment, and that resentment was directed at me.

I was singled out. Mocked. Labeled. I became "the kid whose mom complains," which, in the minds of some teachers, was even worse than being behind in reading. The classroom, already a minefield, became even more hostile. Although I was proud of my mom for standing up for me, I started to hide the toll it was taking. I couldn't let her see how much it hurt. I didn't want her to feel like her efforts were making things worse, even though sometimes they were.

I got even better at pretending.

I masked. At school. At home. Everywhere.

I became an expert at hiding my struggles. I memorized when I couldn't decode. I guessed when I didn't know. I avoided reading aloud, avoided asking questions, avoided drawing attention to myself. I couldn't bear the judgment. My survival strategy was to blend in, to appear fine, to carry the weight quietly. It wasn't about deception. It was about protection. It was about saving the fragile confidence I was just beginning to build.

That silence came at a cost.

It's exhausting to wear a mask every single day. It eats away at your sense of self. It makes you feel like your entire worth depends on how well you can pretend to be someone you're not. That's not education, it's emotional warfare.

Yet, through it all, those Saturday sessions became something sacred. They weren't magic. I didn't walk out one day suddenly fluent in reading, but they chipped away at the wall. Slowly, carefully, brick by brick. I began to understand that while learning might never come easily to me, it wasn't impossible. That realization was more powerful than anything else.

Looking back now, I see just how pivotal those sacrifices were. My mom found hope for me in that tutor. She gave me the kind of belief that no test score could measure. Even on the days I wanted to quit, she kept pushing me forward because she saw what was already in me.

It took years to realize that my dyslexia and ADHD were not things to conceal, but traits to understand and embrace. They've shaped how I think, how I solve problems, how I lead. They've pushed me to work harder, to dig deeper, to defy expectations. Instead of seeing obstacles, I started seeing strategy, like turning a maze into a map while everyone else was still arguing about where the entrance was, I was already running through the maze.

Different isn't dangerous. And it sure as hell isn't broken. It's a different kind of brilliance, one forged in frustration, built with tenacity, and sharpened through years of silent battles most people never see.

If you're still hiding, still duct-taping your confidence together just to get through the day, this chapter is for you. Not because I figured it all out, but because I stopped pretending I needed to.

The world doesn't need more people who fit in.

It needs more people who stand out.

Maybe, just maybe, your difference is the very thing that makes you unstoppable. Being different doesn't mean you have to do it alone. In fact, you can't.

Chapter 4

When the World Thinks You're Broken

School is supposed to be a place of discovery, a launchpad for dreams, a space for kids to grow, fail, get back up, and figure out who they are. For some, it is all that. For me, it was the opposite. My early school years weren't about thriving; they were about surviving. From the very beginning, I was swimming against a current I couldn't see, in a system that had no place for the way my brain worked.

Dyslexia and ADHD weren't well understood in those days. To be honest, they were barely acknowledged. Instead of support, I was met with blank stares, impatient sighs, and too many voices telling me I was broken, or just not trying hard enough. What should've been a foundation for my future turned into a battlefield. Every classroom became a proving ground where I had to fight for the right just to be seen as capable, never mind successful.

That fight shaped me. It toughened me, but it also bruised me in ways that didn't show on the outside. Yes, I developed grit, enough to carry me through things that would've stopped most kids cold. Grit also has a flip side. It became my shield, my way of pushing forward, even when I felt crushed inside. It also meant hiding the truth, hiding the shame, hiding the fear, and the sense that I would never quite measure up. My grit kept me going, but it also wore me down.

Where the Struggle Bus Rolled in and Parked

The real unraveling began in grade school. From the start, reading and writing were battles I couldn't win. My first-grade teacher didn't try to understand. Instead of helping, she humiliated me. She rolled her eyes in front of the class and treated me like a willful rebel instead of a struggling kid. What should've been a safe place to learn became a minefield of anxiety and shame.

That teacher targeted me. Every day felt like a public performance where I was the punchline. And at six years old, you don't question authority. If an adult says you're lazy, you believe it. If they say you're dumb, you absorb it. And I did.

Second grade brought a glimmer of hope. I had a kind, patient teacher who looked past the chaos. For the first time, I wasn't afraid of the adult at the front of the room, but the damage had been done. I carried the fear, anxiety, and self-doubt from the year before like a shadow. Even with kindness, reading and writing were still uphill. The words still danced. The letters still flipped, and the gap between me and my classmates only grew wider.

Oddly, third grade is a total blank. I have no memory of it. Maybe it was too stressful. Or maybe it was finally quiet. The only thing I remember is learning multiplication at home, at my own pace, free from judgment.

Fourth grade began with promise. My teacher in Michigan made learning fun, almost like an adventure. For once, school didn't feel like punishment. But it didn't last. That fall, we moved to Henderson, Nevada, and with that move, came another brutal reminder: I still didn't fit. My new teacher didn't hide her disdain. She openly predicted I'd drop out and end up pumping gas. Later, she stopped my mom at Kmart to ask if I was still close to flunking. Who does that to a kid?

Thankfully, my mom stepped in, and I moved on to fifth grade. But school was no longer about learning. It became a test of endurance.

Fifth grade brought another new school and a kind but passive teacher. I was sent to the "resource room," the place for kids who didn't fit the mold. Being there felt like wearing a neon sign that read: *I don't belong.* I was branded. Even as my mom kept fighting for me, school became less about moving forward and more about not falling farther behind.

Then came sixth grade, still part of elementary school back then. It was by far the worst year for me. My teacher was like a drill sergeant with a mean streak. Aggressive, dismissive, relentless. She'd announce my trips to the resource room like a town crier reading a sentence. Every time she said my name, it stung. My classmates followed her lead. Mocking became normal. And inside me, something began to crack.

That year, the dark thoughts came. I felt isolated and hopeless. I started to wonder if the world would be better without me. I was eleven.

But like a cornered animal, I fought back, not with fists, but with humor. I realized if I could make people laugh, I could deflect. I could shift the spotlight, even for a moment. Humor became my armor. It didn't fix things, but it helped me survive.

Another tool I developed: pretending I didn't care. I let the insults slide, at least on the outside. Inside, they landed hard. But I learned not to show it. If others saw my pain, they had power. So, I smiled, joked, and acted bulletproof. That became my survival.

I became a master of faking confidence. If you can't perform, be funny. If you can't be smart, be cool. If you can't be normal, at least look unfazed. It's a heavy mask to wear. And it teaches you, in quiet, corrosive ways, that your real self isn't worthy.

Through it all, my mom was my rock. My relentless, embarrassing, beautiful force of nature. She argued with teachers, demanded more and better for me, tracked down resources as if her life depended on it, because mine did. I rolled my eyes at her back then. Now, I can see she saved me.

I still remember my fourth-grade teacher predicting I'd become a ditch digger. And I did. I became a professional ditch digger, with a PhD in environmental soil chemistry. So yes, I dig holes… but I do it with scientific precision, thank you very much.

Elementary school didn't just show me how hard the world could be, but it taught me how my brain worked. I didn't have the words yet, but I was figuring out how to adapt. I needed to see things, not just hear them.

So, I started drawing. I broke big assignments into smaller pieces. I tapped my pencil, bounced my leg, paced around the room, because movement helped me think.

Those early years taught me more than most classrooms ever could. They taught me resilience. They taught me that success doesn't always follow straight lines. That being different wasn't a flaw, it was a clue. A clue to hidden strengths I hadn't yet unlocked. My memory. My curiosity. My unrelenting drive. Those were my strengths. I just hadn't learned to use them yet.

Eventually, I did. I created systems. I recorded lectures. I read aloud. I broke information into chunks. I learned to advocate for myself. I found mentors who saw potential where others only saw failure.

I didn't listen to the early voices, the teachers who told me I'd never amount to anything. Instead, I went on to earn Master's and Doctoral degrees, lead scientific research, and become an expert in environmental chemistry and food contamination. I turned every cruel word into fuel.

"I rewrote the story they tried to hand me."

Middle School: Humor and Deflection

But middle school was waiting for me. And it didn't just raise the academic bar; it cranked up the chaos. Seventh grade hit like a wave I couldn't see coming. Juggling seven classes a day may have felt like a rite of passage to some kids, but to me, it was like being thrown into a mental obstacle course with no map, no rope, and no finish line in sight. From the very beginning, I was placed in what the school politely called "Below Average" classes, a label that stuck to my back like duct tape. Translation? You're not good enough.

These weren't nurturing classrooms. They were academic holding pens, where kids like me were shuffled just far enough along to move us out of the way. Most of my teachers were mentally checked out. Their low expectations wrapped around me like a lead blanket. I carried their disappointment like a second backpack, heavier than the first.

In spite of my tutoring for dyslexia, reading and writing were still monumental struggles. Spelling felt like trying to win a spelling bee in another language. Forming full sentences? Like assembling a puzzle where half the pieces were missing, and the rest were upside down. Math wasn't any better. Numbers mocked me from the page. But in shop class? I came alive. Working with my hands gave me something I could finish, something real, something that didn't laugh back at me.

And when the academics failed me, as they often did, I leaned into the one thing I had always had: humor. Then, eventually, creativity. Improvisation. Deflection. All the tools of survival.

In seventh grade, I learned how to juggle. Literally. I smuggled tennis balls into class like they were contraband, and when boredom hit (which, let's be honest, was nearly every period), I'd start casually tossing them into the air behind the teacher's back. My own little circus of one.

But I didn't stop there. That year, I also taught myself how to ride a unicycle. And yes, eventually, I even learned to juggle while riding the unicycle. Because if you're going to be "the weird kid," you might as well go all in.

One day, the inevitable happened. I dropped a ball. Thud. The sound echoed like a warning shot. Thirty heads turned in synchronized judgment. The teacher froze mid-sentence, slowly turned around like a villain about to deliver a monologue, and locked eyes with me, clearly seconds away from launching into a speech that would crush any dreams of a career in circus arts. I froze too, mid-juggle, mid-regret, caught red-handed, one tennis ball still bouncing traitorously across the floor. I remember my home economics teacher, yep, I took that class, asking me why I was juggling, and I said:

"Relax," I said coolly. "I'm just balancing my education."

The class exploded in laughter. The teacher? Not so much. She confiscated my juggling balls, so I got creative, pencils, erasers, apples, and anything I could toss. By year's end, I could juggle almost anything... except homework. Still, juggling taught me something I couldn't learn from a textbook: focus, rhythm, patience, three things I desperately needed to rein in the chaos inside my mind.

I was also slowly building other survival techniques. If a giant assignment felt impossible, I'd break it into smaller parts. Flashcards became my secret weapon—bright colors, bold letters, stick-figure drawings that made words finally mean something. And though humor started as a shield, it became a bridge. If I could make people laugh, I could control the moment. Suddenly I wasn't "the slow kid"—I was the funny kid. And sometimes, that earned me grace when I stumbled.

One teacher, though, was different. A beacon in the fog: Mr. Terry Frosini. He taught English for below-average students, but he never treated us that way. He got it. He gave us space to fail without punishment and introduced me to reading in ways that didn't terrify me, comic books, short stories, anything bite-sized that didn't overwhelm. If writing was too hard, he let me present orally or visually. He saw the kid behind the struggle. And that changed everything.

Unfortunately, eighth grade felt like sliding back down the mountain. Still trapped in the "Below Average" track, I was surrounded by the same low expectations that told me to keep my head down and not expect much. But by then, I had perfected the art of hiding. I jokingly call it my "PhD in humor and deflection." I couldn't spell, sure, but I could deliver a one-liner that would make the whole room erupt. That became my armor.

Underneath the jokes, though, I still felt invisible. I could distract others from my struggles, but I couldn't distract myself from the quiet ache of not belonging.

That year, I started learning how to advocate for myself, just a little. I'd ask teachers, "Can I do a presentation instead of a paper?" Sometimes they said no. But sometimes they surprised me and said yes. Those small wins mattered. I also discovered the magic of repetition. I'd read something aloud, record it onto a cassette, then play it back over and over. Hearing it helped far more than seeing it. It gave me a new way in.

But middle school doesn't care about your coping strategies.

One day in eighth-grade English, my nightmare became real: I was called on to read aloud. The words twisted and blurred. I stumbled. I stuttered. Laughter erupted, not the kind I orchestrated. This time, it was at me. I wanted to disappear.

The lesson was about future careers. Through burning cheeks and trembling lips, I said, "I want to be a veterinarian."

The teacher raised her eyebrows. A few kids snickered.

One kid blurted out "You'll have no patients!"

I wasn't about to let it slide. So, I fired back:

"I'll have one patient—and that'll be your mother."

Boom. The class howled. Even the teacher tried to hide their smile. That kid slumped in his seat, seething, and I stood tall, not because I'd won an argument, but because I'd used my hidden strengths to take back the moment. That wasn't the first time I'd flipped the script, and it wouldn't be the last.

I had a whole act by then. My Roast of the Year routine was basically an unsanctioned stand-up special that broke out anytime the class dragged. Still, there was always one kid who thought he could out-joke me. One day during science, he piped up:

"Hey, you know you're not as funny as you think you are, right?"

I leaned back, grinned, and replied:

"And you know you're not as smart as your mom thinks you are, right?"

The room detonated. Even the teacher cracked up behind the textbook. That kid never tried me again. And I learned something valuable: if you could make the teacher laugh too, you won the room.

Sure, it sometimes came with consequences, like cleaning lockers after school. But it was worth it.

Academically, the grind never let up. Reading and writing were still mountains. Math felt like trying to decode ancient hieroglyphics. The "Below Average" label stuck. The isolation stuck. And so did the sarcasm.

I had one reliable weapon: my mouth. When someone took a jab at me, I could slice back twice as fast. It started as defense. But eventually, it became offense. I could embarrass people without even thinking about it. I wasn't trying to be mean, but in survival mode, kindness isn't the first priority. You don't think about what your shield might be doing to others.

Even outside of school, fitting in wasn't easy. I wasn't ugly, but my fashion sense was a disaster. Outdated clothes, mismatched outfits, symptoms of a lower-middle-class budget and parents who weren't exactly Vogue subscribers. It made me an easy target. I didn't stand out for anything great, not grades, not confidence, just awkward clothes and fast comebacks.

Deflection wasn't just a tactic, it was my personality. Sarcasm, quick wit, and clowning around were how I got through each day. But the mask came at a cost. I didn't realize it then, but I was keeping everyone, even the people who cared, at arm's length. I thought I was being clever. I thought I was surviving. But I was also hiding.

And the truth I didn't realize until years later: my words could hurt. Just like theirs hurt me. I didn't want to be cruel. I just wanted to not be crushed. But in building my armor, I sometimes threw daggers.

Middle school didn't give me grades to hang on the fridge. It gave me grit. It gave me survival instincts. And it taught me to find power in laughter. Humor saved me. But it also kept me hidden.

I didn't know it yet, but that balance, between armor and honesty, would take me years to figure out.

Middle School: Dodging Disaster and Awkwardness

Middle school didn't get easier, but I got smarter. Not in the academic sense, at least not the way schools measure it. But smarter in how I handled myself. Smarter in how I faced the uphill climb of dyslexia and ADHD. Despite the ongoing battles, something shifted inside me during those years. I stopped seeing school as something I had to endure and started figuring out how to survive it; on my terms.

It became clear pretty quickly that the system wasn't built for kids like me. The educational system was content to push students along, pass them forward, whether they learned anything or not. No one was coming to save me. Teachers didn't expect much. A few even told me, flat-out, "You'll never graduate," as if I was destined for failure. One said, "Life's going to be hard for a kid like you." Maybe they thought they were preparing me for reality. But what they didn't know was that somewhere deep inside, I'd already made a decision:

They don't get to write my story. I do.

During those years, I started developing tools that would carry me through life. Not test-taking strategies but practical, hard-earned, life-tested methods. These weren't tricks. They were survival skills. They were how I clawed my way through school, and they're still with me today. If you've ever felt like the system wasn't built for you either, maybe these will help you too.

The first thing I learned was how to break big problems into small ones. A ten-page paper? No chance. But ten short paragraphs? That I could do. I'd chip away at them one at a time. A mountain of vocabulary words? I'd turn them into flashcards, color-coded, bite-sized, digestible. No all-nighters, no cramming. Just short bursts, taken in pieces I could manage. I learned that finishing something small was a hell of a lot better than giving up on something big.

Repetition became my secret weapon. Reading silently didn't stick. But reading out loud? That worked. I'd read a paragraph into a cassette recorder, then play it back over and over, on my Walkman, in bed, riding my bike, anywhere. I didn't care how strange it looked. I was building my own way of learning. If you can't learn one way, find another. Your brain is trying to help you; it just needs you to listen to what actually works.

Another breakthrough came when I stopped trying to memorize facts and started turning them into stories or pictures. My brain didn't just like visuals, it needed them. I'd turn information into drawings, mental images, even little comics in the margins of my notes. If I couldn't remember the parts of a plant cell, I'd turn them into characters in a Saturday morning cartoon. The mitochondria became the "muscle guy," chloroplasts wore sunglasses. It sounds ridiculous, but it worked.

Sometimes I'd act it out. Movement helped me think. If I was studying something tough, I'd pace around the room, bounce a tennis ball, anything to keep my body in sync with my brain. If reading didn't click, I drew. If drawing didn't click, I moved. I discovered the key wasn't to force one method, it was to stay flexible. There's no one way to learn. There's just the way that works for you.

I also learned to grow thicker skin. Not because words stopped hurting, but because I decided they didn't get to control me. The teasing, the low expectations, the casual cruelty from classmates and teachers, it still stung. It always stung. But I taught myself to let it roll off, at least on the outside. Like water on the hood of a car. Not because I didn't feel it, but because reacting gave them the upper hand. Staying calm meant I kept the power.

I realized something else along the way, something big. Resilience isn't a trait. It's a habit.

It's not some heroic quality you're born with. It's built one tiny act at a time. Every time I wanted to quit but didn't, that was resilience. Every time I failed, then stood up and tried again, I was stacking bricks of self-belief. Eventually, I had built something solid, something no teacher, no bully, no system could take from me.

Outside of school, that resilience came alive in an entirely different way.

My neighborhood friends and I turned mischief into an art form. We were legends on our block, masters of ding-dong ditch, water-balloon warfare, and the *pièce de résistance*: the flaming bag of dog poop. Yes, *that* one. We didn't just cause trouble, we engineered it. Schematics. Escape routes. Code names. We were prankster Einsteins with a knack for chaos and a love for the dramatic.

In those moments, I wasn't the kid who struggled to read or couldn't spell "Wednesday" without getting lost halfway through. I was fearless. Clever. Bold. Free.

And yeah, those hijinks may sound ridiculous now, but they gave me something school never did, confidence. Out there, I wasn't broken, I was brave. No one cared if I failed a spelling test. What mattered was whether I could duck behind a bush before Mr. Henderson found out it was us again. I was just a kid living in the moment, laughing so hard it hurt, knowing I could outrun any yelling adult and probably negotiate my way out of grounding, too.

And maybe that's the most important lesson I took from middle school: learning doesn't just happen in classrooms with chalkboards and Scantrons. Sometimes it happens in the streets, on front lawns, or mid-prank when your getaway plan goes sideways. That's where I started learning who I really was, how my brain worked, what I needed to feel alive, and what kind of strength it took to survive when the world kept trying to tell you you'd never make it.

They thought I'd never graduate.

They thought I'd never succeed.

But I wasn't living by their playbook anymore.

I started writing my own, and let's just say… mine has way better plot twists.

The Tools That Got Me Through

Looking back now, it's easy to assume there was some kind of plan, that I had a strategy, a blueprint, a clear path forward. I didn't. What I had was chaos, pain, and a deep, burning refusal to give up. And from that, I built a toolbox.

Not the kind you carry with a handle and hinges. This was a mental, emotional, survival-based set of tools, forged not in comfort but in classrooms filled with judgment, playgrounds lined with cruelty, and long nights wrestling with the kind of self-doubt that swallows kids whole. I didn't sit down one day and decide to be resourceful. I was backed into corners, called names, underestimated, and I fought back the only way I knew how: by adapting.

Some of those tools started as desperate coping mechanisms, little things I did just to stay afloat. But over time, they became who I am. They shaped how I think, how I learn, how I lead, and how I thrive. And decades later, I still use every one of them.

Humor as Armor

I couldn't read out loud without stumbling. I couldn't spell "because" even if you held a dictionary to my head and whispered the letters. But I could make people laugh. Fast. Before anyone had the chance to point at my mistakes, I'd beat them to the punchline and throw in a rimshot for good measure. Humor became my shield, my deflection, my survival tactic. If I could get the room to laugh with me, maybe they wouldn't laugh at me.

And in those moments, those quick, witty saves, I felt seen. Not for what I couldn't do, but for something I could. Something that wasn't on any test but still felt like a kind of strength. Even if I was failing spelling, at least I was passing comedy.

Building Thick Skin

Letting cruel words bounce off me didn't come naturally. It hurt. But I learned that reacting only gave the bullies and the jaded teachers more fuel. So, I acted like I didn't care. And every time I refused to flinch, I got a little stronger. Not invincible—but stronger. Thick skin isn't about not feeling. It's about choosing the feelings you show to others.

Breaking Big Problems into Small Pieces

No one ever taught me how to manage overwhelming tasks. I had to figure that out on my own. Ten-page paper? That might as well have been a novel. But one paragraph at a time? That I could do. Vocabulary lists turned into flashcards. Assignments got split into bite-sized tasks. Every little win gave me the momentum to keep going. I learned that progress isn't about speed, it's about not stopping.

Visual Learning and Storytelling

The words on a textbook page might as well have been Greek. But pictures? I could remember those. Diagrams, doodles, ridiculous mnemonics that made no sense to anyone else but clicked in my brain, those became my secret weapons. If a fact didn't stick, I'd turn it into a story. I made science into cartoons, history into movie scenes, math into puzzles. My brain needed visuals, so I gave it what it craved.

Repetition in New Forms

Reading silently was like trying to absorb water with a rock. It didn't work. I changed the method. I read out loud, recorded myself on cheap cassette tapes, and listened back while riding my bike or lying in bed. It wasn't high-tech, but it worked. I learned the same thing over and over until it stuck. If one method failed, I tried another. I didn't quit. I adjusted.

Movement to Focus

Sitting still? Not happening. My brain wanted motion. So instead of fighting it, I made movement part of how I learned. Tapping a pencil, bouncing my leg, pacing the room, I turned what looked like fidgeting into focus. Movement wasn't my distraction. It was my bridge to attention.

Self-Advocacy (in Small Doses)

I wasn't ready to stand on a desk and demand accommodations. But I learned to speak up in small ways. "Can I give a presentation instead of writing a paper?" "Can I draw this instead of write it?" Sometimes teachers said no. But sometimes they said yes. And those small victories reminded me that asking matters. That my voice, even shaky, had value.

Improvisation and Quick Thinking

Juggling in class. Tossing out one-liners. Turning a humiliating moment into a punchline. I learned how to think on my feet, because I had to. Quick wit wasn't just for fun; it was survival. Improvisation helped me stay one step ahead of the judgment. Sometimes it saved my day. Sometimes it saved my dignity.

Turning Criticism into Fuel

"You'll never graduate." "You won't make it." Those weren't just insults. They were matches, and I collected them. Every word that was supposed to break me became kindling. They didn't defeat me. They lit a fire I still carry today. I didn't confront those teachers. I didn't need to. Success became my rebuttal.

Finding Outlets to Be Myself

In the classroom, I was the kid with the red pen of failure hanging over my head. But outside, I was a prankster, a schemer, a goofball with no leash. Ding-dong ditch, water balloons, flaming bags on porches, those weren't just stunts. They were released. Out there, I wasn't struggling. I was thriving. I wasn't being graded; I was being me. Fearless. Fast. Fun. Free.

None of these tools came from a textbook. No one taught them to me. They were built through failure, refined in frustration, and sharpened by necessity. They were my response to a world that told me I couldn't. And every time I used one, I proved that I could.

So, if you're out there right now, sitting in the back of a classroom, staring at a blank page, wondering if you'll ever measure up, listen closely: Your toolbox is already a work in progress, too.

Every time you fail and try again, you're crafting something powerful. Every insult you rise above, every obstacle you rework, every moment you refuse to quit, you're building tools no one can take away from you.

And maybe the most important lesson of all?

You don't have to fit someone else's mold. You just have to keep going. One small, determined step at a time.

Your way forward doesn't have to be perfect.

It must be yours.

Teachers' Reactions and Coping Mechanisms

Middle school was supposed to be a time of transition, of growth, of discovering who you are. For me, it was a series of subtle betrayals by people who were supposed to believe in me.

By then, I had already internalized that I was different, that learning wasn't easy for me, that I had to work harder just to keep up. But instead of encouragement or support, many of my teachers offered something far more damaging: indifference. They didn't threaten to hold me back like in elementary school. No, middle school teachers had a different tactic, grim predictions delivered with a shrug.

"You'll never graduate from high school, Doug"

They'd say,

"Life is going to be tough for you"

What's a kid supposed to do with that? At twelve years old, hearing an adult tell you to prepare for failure doesn't feel like guidance. It feels like surrender. And not your surrender, their own. It's as if they'd already written my story, sealed it, and stamped it: Return to sender, Not Worth the Effort.

There wasn't any real attempt to understand my learning challenges. Dyslexia? ADHD? It might as well have been ancient Greek to them. These weren't viewed as learning differences; they were treated like character flaws. The goal wasn't to help students like me thrive; it was to move us along, just enough to get us out of the way.

And unlike a punch to the gut, these blows didn't knock the wind out of me all at once. They came quietly, in tired voices and condescending tones. They were slow leaks in the balloon of my confidence.

It's easy, in hindsight, to recognize that those words came from teachers battling their own frustrations, their own lack of training or burnout. But as a child, I didn't know that. I didn't know how to tell the difference between someone's personal baggage and my own worth.

I just knew it hurt.

The damage wasn't always loud. It was subtle. It was in the way a teacher's eyes skimmed over me when they asked a question. The sigh when I raised my hand. The barely disguised frustration when I turned in work that didn't meet their idea of "normal." They weren't building me up. They were writing me off.

They didn't say it with concern. They said it as if it were already decided, a formality. A sentence, not a conversation. Like my future had been stamped and filed away before I even had a chance to live it.

For a kid already drowning in self-doubt, it wasn't just discouraging, it was crushing. Their voices became the narrator in my mind, following me into every classroom, every test, every report card.

But here's what they didn't count on: I was stubborn. Somewhere inside, a small spark refused to go out. I couldn't explain it then, but I had an instinct to push back, even if it was silent at first.

Their inability to see my potential didn't mean it wasn't there. They weren't measuring me; they were revealing their limitations.

So, I turned their doubt into fuel.

Every time someone told me I wouldn't succeed, I stored it. Their words became my internal engine, played back on repeat when I was tired, lost, or ready to quit. Those voices weren't prophetic, they were wrong. I didn't need perfect teachers. I didn't need praise. What I needed was resilience. Self-belief. Grit. The kind that keeps you walking forward when the world tells you to sit down.

If you've ever been told, "You won't make it," remember this: they don't get to decide. Only you know what you're capable of. Their doubt has no power unless you hand it to them. The only voice that matters is your own, the one that whispers, keep going, even when everything else tells you to stop. You don't have to be the best. You don't have to be perfect. You just have to keep showing up. Keep trying. Keep believing in the version of yourself that no one else can see yet. Because one day, you may just become that person.

Emotional and Social Challenges

Emotionally, middle school was a storm I wasn't prepared for, the kind that doesn't strike all at once but seeps in slowly with every smirk, every lowered expectation, every teacher who had already given up on me. Over time, the message became clear: you're not going anywhere, kid. And the worst part? I started to believe it.

I tried to laugh it off. I hid behind sarcasm and pranks. But inside, it was wearing me down, quietly shaping the way I saw myself.

One moment from eighth grade still replays in my mind like it happened yesterday. I was in world geography class when the teacher called on me to read aloud. My stomach dropped. My mouth went dry. I was reading at a fourth-grade level, and nothing sends a dyslexic kid into panic like being told to read in front of thirty classmates.

Still, I stood up.

I tried.

But every word was a battlefield. I stumbled. I paused. I mispronounced. My face burned. My hands shook. And just when I thought it couldn't get worse, the teacher cut in, voice sharp, dripping with judgment:

"How did you make it to eighth grade when you can't even read simple words?"

The room erupted in laughter.

Not the kind you share. The kind that cuts. The kind that tells you: You are the joke.

I stood there, frozen, holding back tears with everything I had. Not because I didn't want to cry, I did, but because I knew if I did, it would only make it worse. The humiliation was total. It wasn't just a moment of embarrassment; it was a message. A message that said: You don't belong here. You're not worth the effort. Trying doesn't matter.

The shame followed me into every classroom. I didn't just fear failure, I feared being seen. I became an expert in invisibility, praying not to be called on, doing everything I could to survive the day without being exposed.

Anxiety and shame became my daily companions. Learning stopped being about curiosity, it became about survival.

But pain isn't always the end. Sometimes, it's the beginning of something else. I didn't know it then, but that humiliating moment in geography class became part of the foundation I would stand on years later. It didn't break me. It built me. Slowly, painfully, it gave me grit. It gave me clarity. It taught me that no one, not a teacher, not a diagnosis, not a room full of laughing classmates, gets to decide who I am.

That moment didn't define me. It refined me. And it became the spark that ignited everything that came next.

High School—Perfecting the Mask

My transition into high school was less of a step forward and more of a stumble into deeper uncertainty. The first quarter was a disaster. I failed nearly every class. Every subject felt like it was in a language I couldn't decode. And before I could catch my breath, I was moved into Special Education, small, self-contained classrooms with eight to ten students, all labeled like me.

The room was anything but a sanctuary or a safe space for learning. It felt like a holding tank. A place to store the kids who didn't "fit." Some of my classmates had learning disabilities, like me. Others were there because of behavioral issues. And then there were kids like the one who I understand, in hindsight, had severe mental health issues, complete with near-daily, frightening outbursts requiring removal from the classroom.

Sadly, this was typical for Special Education in the 1980s. This was my "support system."

It was in the 9th grade that I was handed something called an Individualized Education Program, an IEP. On paper, it was supposed to help. It was a plan, tailored just for me. Accommodations. Modifications. Support. That's what they called it.

But to me? It felt like a confirmation that I had been officially stamped: Different. Less Than. A project to manage, not a person to believe in.

It wasn't a moment of relief; it was a quiet sentence. A formal declaration of limitations.

The teachers didn't pretend otherwise. One told me plainly,

"You're probably not going to finish high school."

I nodded like I didn't care, like it didn't hurt—but I carried that comment for a long time. It echoed every time I failed a quiz. Every time I felt lost in a lesson. Every time I overheard someone call us "the dumb kids."

Oddly enough, this was also when some of my old habits, the pranks, the mischief, the late-night adventures with friends, started to fade. Not because of some grand moral epiphany. No one sat me down and inspired change. I was just exhausted. School was draining me. Surviving each day took everything I had. There wasn't energy left for goofing off after the bell.

My friend circle changed, too. The kids I ran around with in middle school weren't part of my world anymore. High school brought new faces, new energies, new perspectives. These kids had goals. Plans. Some even talked about college like it was a real thing, not a fantasy. I started to wonder if maybe, somehow, there was still a version of the future where I didn't end up exactly where they predicted.

High school was still hard, don't get me wrong. It was a daily grind. But for the first time, I began to feel a flicker of possibility. A small, defiant voice in the back of my head saying: What if they're wrong? What if you're not done yet?

Still, being in special education classes carried a weight that most people can't understand unless they've worn it. As a teenager trying desperately to figure out who I was, trying to shape some version of an identity I could be proud of, the stigma was brutal. I did everything I could to hide it.

It felt like wearing a scarlet letter.

I took long detours through hallways to avoid being seen going into the Special Ed wing. I'd time my entry to avoid passing crowds. If someone asked what class I was headed to, I'd change the subject or make up a name that sounded more "normal." The fear of being found out was constant. Every interaction felt like a performance, like I was walking a tightrope over a pit of judgment.

The emotional toll of it all was relentless. Every dismissive glance, every time a teacher spoke slowly to me like I couldn't keep up, every time a classmate made an offhand comment like "Oh, that's the dumb class, right?" It added another brick to the weight I was carrying.

And the worst part? I didn't push back. I didn't defend myself. I just absorbed it all in silence.

Because I thought maybe they were right.

That's what low expectations do. They don't just limit you on paper, they shrink your world from the inside out. And no matter how much you try to fake confidence, it's hard to grow when everyone around you expects you to fail.

Here's the truth: that story they wrote for me? I didn't sign it.

I started rewriting it, not with perfect grades or overnight success, but with something better: refusal. Refusal to let their assumptions be my outcome. Refusal to stay quiet. Refusal to disappear.

Because deep down, even buried under all that shame, was a part of me that still believed I was capable of more.

And that belief, that spark, was about to become the most important thing I had.

Building My High School Survival Toolkit

High school didn't wave a magic wand and make everything easier. If anything, the expectations were steeper, the judgments sharper, and the stakes felt enormous. But by that point, I'd already survived the emotional gauntlet of middle school. I wasn't about to let the next chapter write me off. Instead of letting those pressures crush me, I started crafting something of my own, a set of strategies, survival tools, little victories strung together like lifelines. These weren't hacks I read in a book. These were forged in late-night panic, hallway humiliation, and a stubborn refusal to go quietly.

Speaking Up for Myself

By the time I hit high school, I'd figured something out: no one was going to swoop in and offer me accommodations unless I asked. I asked. I learned to advocate for myself, timidly at first, then louder. "Can I do a presentation instead of writing a paper?" "Could I get extra time?" Not every teacher said yes, but enough of them did. And every yes reminded me that my voice mattered, that I had some control over how I learned, even if I had to fight for it.

Tackling Big Assignments in Pieces

A ten-page paper might as well have been Everest. But I learned to chip away at it. One paragraph. One sentence. One bullet point. I rewarded myself with breaks, snacks, music, tiny wins to keep momentum alive. It wasn't elegant, but it worked. And when things felt too big, I just made them smaller.

Leaning Into Visual and Hands-On Learning

Forget forcing myself to cram from a book. That was a waste of time and mental energy I didn't have. Instead, I turned to diagrams, color-coded flashcards, mind maps, and models. If I could see it or build it, I could understand it. I stopped trying to learn the way I was told and started learning the way that worked for me.

Repetition with a Twist

Reading silently was like shouting into a void. It never stuck. I started reading out loud, sometimes to myself, sometimes to a tape recorder. I'd listen to those recordings over and over, especially on the bus or while pacing around the garage. It felt ridiculous at first, but it worked. Hearing the material helped lock it in.

Movement as Focus Fuel

By this point, I stopped trying to "sit still and concentrate." That was never going to happen. Instead, I embraced the movement. Flashcards while pacing. Bouncing a ball while reviewing notes. Tapping a foot, drumming on the desk. My brain worked better when my body wasn't trapped.

Finding Quiet Spaces

Focus didn't come naturally; I had to engineer it. I sought out corners of the library, quiet spots at home, any place I could shut out the noise and create some mental clarity. It wasn't about silence; it was about control.

Thick Skin and Mental Reframing

The cruel comments? The low expectations? They didn't stop. But I stopped letting them define me. I reframed the narrative. Every insult became a challenge. Every "you can't" became a dare: Watch me.

Quick Thinking and Improvisation

I learned to think fast. Humor became my defense and my weapon. If I could deflect with a joke or a quick comeback, I could control the moment. I used it to navigate everything, from classroom chaos to cafeteria politics.

Flexibility and Adaptability

If one method didn't work, I tried another. High school didn't hand out instruction manuals, so I made my own. I learned to pivot, to adjust, to adapt, because getting stuck wasn't an option.

Resilience in the Face of Failure

And most of all, I built resilience. Not the glossy, Instagram-inspirational quote-over-a-mountain-sunset kind. I'm talking about real resilience, the kind you earn when you bomb a test, ugly-cry in your car while clutching a burrito and still show up the next day. Every time I got back up, I just didn't survive, I leveled up. Quiet, unshakeable, and 100% earned.

These weren't academic strategies; they were survival tools. And they didn't just get me through high school; they became the blueprint for adulting. Real adulting. Like, "guess I'll file an extension on my taxes and keep it moving" adulting.

Now, I won't lie and pretend it was smooth. Every single one of those tools was born out of struggle, trial, error, and a few dramatic meltdowns involving textbooks and snacks. I wanted to quit more times than I could count. I fantasized about launching my algebra book into the sun. With force. Preferably during a full moon.

But through all the mess, the misfires, and my own stubborn brain, those tools started to stick.

A Beacon and a Battleground

For someone as socially awkward and insecure as I was, dragging around the weight of dyslexia, ADHD, and the daily bruises of academic failure, the United States Marine Corps JROTC program became both a refuge… and a combat zone. At the start of ninth grade, I opted for the JROTC program over gym, thinking it would be a fun alternative. I had no idea what I was walking into, but I was desperate for somewhere to belong. Somewhere I could be something other than "the dumb kid." Somewhere my weaknesses didn't follow me into every room like an uninvited guest who wouldn't stop pointing out I'd failed another quiz.

JROTC wasn't just another class, it was a tribe. A gloriously ragtag crew of misfits and underdogs. We found each other in those echoing hallways and during pre-sunrise drills when no one else in their right mind was awake. Our bond was forged in sweat, sarcasm, and the kind of shared frustration that only comes from marching in formation with zero coordination.

We weren't perfect. Not even close. We fought. We tripped over our own feet. We lost our tempers, lost our place in line, occasionally lost entire uniforms. But for the first time, I wasn't alone in the struggle. In all our dysfunction, we found connection. In our chaos, we found something that almost resembled belonging. We didn't start out looking for our people, but somewhere between barking cadences and swapping jokes during push-ups, we became each other's lifeline.

But beneath that camaraderie, underneath the laughter and the inside jokes, there was a darker truth. One we didn't talk about much, but we all felt. The three retired Marines who ran the program weren't just teaching discipline. They enforced control with the kind of cold, calculated cruelty that didn't leave bruises, but left scars. For the chosen few, the golden cadets, it was a golden ticket. Praise. Mentorship. Leadership roles. Futures so bright they needed aviators.

But the rest of us? We were background noise. Cannon fodder in the high school version of boot camp. Disposable. Reminded constantly that we weren't "leadership material." If you didn't fit the mold, you were sidelined, punished, mocked, and quietly erased. And for all the strength I found in my peers, the message from the top was clear: some of us mattered. And some of us didn't.

Still, I stayed. Because even in that broken system, we found each other. And that, more than any ribbon or rank, was what kept me showing up.

The Senior Military Instructor, a Colonel with the charm of a door hinge, treated me like malfunctioning equipment, useful only when convenient, and otherwise ignored. He didn't yell much. His silence was worse. It told me I wasn't even worth shouting at.

But the Sergeant Major? He was loud, aggressive, relentless, and not in the motivational, Marine-movie way. No, his goal wasn't to build us up. It was to break us down, one cruel word at a time.

"Get used to being lower than whale shit, Sims."

He said it often. Said it loud. Said it so the whole squad could hear. No one stood up for me. Not because they agreed with him, but because we all knew the rules. Speak up, and you're next. I didn't blame them. We were all walking a tightrope in combat boots.

"Sims, your initials 'DS' stand for Dumb Shit."

Then there was the third instructor, the Master Gunnery Sergeant. His presence was different. Not louder. Not crueler. Just more unsettling. His behavior around the female cadets made us all shift uncomfortably. We'd see the way his eyes lingered, hear the whispers, watch the way his hands "accidentally" found their way to places they never should have. He crossed lines. We all knew it. We were teenagers, not fools. But we were also kids, stuck under the thumbs of men with absolute authority and no accountability.

"You are a total waste of space and energy, Sims."

Today, that kind of behavior would be exposed, investigated, shut down. Back then? It was brushed aside, buried beneath a rigid chain of command and a culture of silence. No one protected us. We did the only thing we could: we protected each other.

Somehow, in that broken system, we cadets formed something real. When the adults failed us, we leaned harder into each other. We trained together. Marched in sync. Covered for one another. And in that strange space between fear and loyalty, we built a kind of family. A messy, dysfunctional one, but real all the same.

Still, the damage was done. Those men, with their clipped words and clipped egos, tore chunks out of what little self-esteem I had left. Every insult, every dismissal, every look of disdain etched deeper into my skin. And the worst part? I believed them. Their cruelty didn't shock me, it confirmed everything I already feared about myself. That I wasn't good enough. That I didn't belong. That I was destined to fail.

But here's the twist.

JROTC, for all its pain and betrayal, also gave me a gift. Not from the instructors, but in spite of them. It taught me how not to lead. It showed me what power looks like when it's rotten. What authority becomes when it's wielded without compassion. Those men thought they were instilling discipline. What they really taught me was this: when leadership is built on fear, it's not leadership at all. It's abuse.

And though I didn't realize it at the time, something inside me hardened, not into bitterness, but resolve. A quiet fire. A whispered vow. If I ever held authority, if I ever stood in front of a room with influence, I would never treat people the way they treated us. I would never lead through fear, shame, or silence.

I would lead differently.

Because even back then, broken and scared as I was, I knew there had to be a better way.

The Impact of Verbal Abuse

The relentless verbal attacks weren't occasional, they were daily. At first, they hit like open wounds, each one sharp and immediate. Then I tried convincing myself I was numb to them. That maybe, just maybe, they slid off me like rain on a coat. But they didn't. They stuck like barbed wire, each one embedding deeper than the last. Especially the ones from the Sergeant Major. His cruelty wasn't spontaneous. It was precise. Deliberate. Sharpened with intent.

"Sims, you couldn't lead ants to sugar."

I still hear his voice. That tone, dry, acidic, laced with contempt. It didn't matter how hard I tried. How often I showed up. How much sweat I poured onto that drill pad. I could've marched myself into the ground, and in his eyes, I'd still be less than nothing. He didn't just want me to follow orders; he wanted to erase me.

"I've seen bricks with more potential than you."

I never told my family. How do you say that out loud? That the one place you thought might finally give you structure, pride, purpose… became just another place to be torn apart? I figured if I said it, I'd be giving his words more power. Or worse, confirming they were real. So, I swallowed it. All of it.

And yet, JROTC wasn't all shadows. There was structure in that chaos. Routine in the madness. And in that gray zone between drill and dismissal, I found my people. In hindsight, I think we were misfits, the outliers, the kids with chipped armor and duct-taped confidence. We didn't talk much about our pain, but we felt it in each other. We are stuck together. Whispered jokes during inspections. Shared glances when someone got chewed out. Covered for each other when the walls closed in.

"You'll never amount to anything but a disappointment."

But I never let myself relax. I couldn't. I filled the silence with sarcasm and jokes. I could make the whole battalion laugh, including, occasionally, the instructors. That laughter? It was a brief win. Until it came with punishment. Push-ups until my arms gave out. Rifle drills until my shoulders shook. Laps until my lungs screamed for air. But none of it hurt more than what sat beneath it: that no matter what I did, I was still that kid. The joke. The screw-up. The disappointment.

I remember finishing one of those punishing sessions and sitting alone in the locker room. Staring down at my scuffed boots. Trying to figure out what was so wrong with me. Why couldn't I be good enough? Why couldn't I earn even an ounce of respect from the men who were supposed to shape me?

The worst part wasn't the yelling. It wasn't the push-ups or the laps. It was starting to believe them.

"I've seen rocks with more possibilities than you."

The words didn't bounce off me. I stood at attention. I locked my eyes forward. I did what I was supposed to do. But every one of those insults carved something away inside me.

But the cadets… they saw something else in me. Determination. Loyalty. Maybe even heart. They knew I wouldn't quit, even if my spirit was hanging on by a thread. When the adults saw nothing, my fellow cadets saw me. And sometimes, that was the only thing that kept me standing.

Living with dyslexia and ADHD in that environment was like running underwater. Every step took twice the effort; every instruction came in scrambled signals. The classroom was one battlefield. JROTC was another, with louder consequences. I wasn't just falling behind in school; I was fighting to breathe in a system designed to crush kids who learned like me.

I knew I was trying. But nobody else seemed to see that. Teachers didn't. Instructors didn't. They only saw what I couldn't do. Not the effort. Just the stumbles. Words refused to stay still on the page. Instructions that other kids grasped instantly took me twice as long. My brain ran sprints while everyone else jogged calmly in formation.

And sitting still? Absolute torture. But when I was allowed to move, march, drill, run, the fog in my head cleared. Movement became my anchor. My brain clicked into place when my body did.

I adapted because I had to. No one was going to slow down for me. I leaned into repetition. If I didn't get it the first time, or the fifth, I read it out loud. Paced. Recited it. Over and over. I broke everything into parts. Drill sequences became small commands. I mimicked movements. Watched. Practiced. Repeated. Until my body remembered what my brain couldn't hold.

Those became my lifelines.

But the hardest battle wasn't the Sergeant Major. It wasn't the failing grades. It wasn't the learning curve. It was that voice in my own head. The one that sounded an awful lot like his.

Every day, I fought that voice. The one that said I was broken. The one that echoed:

"Bricks have more potential."

I told myself it didn't matter. But it did. And late at night, or alone after drill, those words echoed louder than anything else. I sat in silence, staring at the floor, wondering why I wasn't enough. Why all my effort seemed invisible.

"You're a disappointment."

I became a master at hiding the cracks. Push it down. Lock it up. Just get through the next minute, the next hour, the next day. I lived in compartments, pain in one, performance in the other. No room to fall apart. No room to be weak.

But even with all of that… I showed up. Every damn day. I didn't quit. I didn't give him the satisfaction. Maybe I didn't believe in myself yet. But I wasn't going to hand over the fight.

Looking back now, I see it for what it was. A war zone dressed up as a leadership program. But the tools I built there, out of desperation, out of necessity, became the very strategies that shaped my future. Dyslexia and ADHD forced me to build a different kind of brain. One wired for adaptation. One fueled by grit.

No, I didn't thrive. I endured.

But sometimes, enduring is the very place where resilience is born.

Reflection: Lessons from the Past

Looking back now, I know without a doubt that the behavior of those instructors in JROTC would never fly today. Their actions didn't just cross lines, they trampled over them. Lines no adult in a position of trust should ever dare to breach. In today's world, they'd be reported, held accountable, and removed. That thought brings a small flicker of justice, but it doesn't erase what those years took from me. The bruises might have been invisible, but they lingered just the same.

And yet I learned. And in the most unlikely place, I found something precious. I found my people.

My fellow cadets weren't just classmates in uniform; they were my crew. My lifeline. My family, at a time when everything else felt like a battlefield, including basic algebra. They didn't roll their eyes when I stumbled through reading aloud. They didn't mock the extra time it took me to memorize a drill or figure out which direction "left" was (don't judge me, it's harder under pressure). They saw me. They saw the sweat, the fight, the fire I dragged into every challenge like a kid trying to prove he belonged, and they celebrated every single win like it was the Olympics.

And let me tell you, those small victories? They were gold. Those were the moments that kept me going. When I nailed a drill, remembered my speech, or didn't trip over my own shoelaces during inspection, it felt like I'd just defied gravity. And my people noticed. Every time.

Because those friendships taught me something no classroom, textbook, or grumpy staff sergeant ever could: you can't do this alone. You need people. The ones who believe in you when you're 100% sure you're broken beyond repair. The ones who prop you up when you're dragging both feet and your dignity. The ones who look past the mess and say, "Hey, you're still standing. That counts."

Tragedy Strikes

Okay, back to my brother's story.

Just when I thought I couldn't carry one more ounce of sorrow, the unthinkable happened.

In the middle of my tenth-grade year, tragedy slammed into my life and shattered what little was left of my stability. My seventeen-year-old brother died suddenly. I was fifteen. We were close in age, but even closer in bond. He was one of the few constants in my life, one of the few people who truly understood me, who made space for me when the world felt too small.

Losing him didn't just break my heart, it cracked the very foundation I was standing on. There's no preparing for that kind of loss and no armor thick enough. One moment, I was barely surviving school, fending off the daily barrage of doubt and ridicule. The next, I was adrift in grief so raw it stole my breath.

Everything that hurt before, the shame, the isolation, and the failures, now all hurt more. And the ground beneath me, the little piece I had managed to stake out for myself, gave way.

The days after his death are a blur of disbelief and rage. I remember the numbness. I remember people talking as if I were in the room, but I wasn't. I remember walking through school hallways like a ghost. I remember teachers saying nothing, and others saying too much. I remember wondering how the world kept spinning when mine had come to a full stop.

I'll return to my brother's death later in this story because, as painful as it was, that loss became a turning point, one that, though I couldn't have known it then, would shape me in powerful ways down the road.

So, I wasn't just dealing with learning struggles or bullying or humiliation anymore; I was trying to process a kind of grief that no fifteen-year-old should ever have to feel.

I was lost.

There's no inspirational bow to tie around that moment. No immediate bounce back. No sudden realization. There was just pain, a deep, hollow ache that made everything else in my life, the jokes, the comebacks, the masks I wore, felt like paper in the rain.

Looking back now, I see just how close I came to letting it all go. I don't mean a dramatic collapse, I mean the slow, suffocating kind of giving up. The kind where your heart doesn't break all at once but wears thin over time until there is nothing left to give. The grief from losing my brother, the shame from school, the daily judgments from people who were supposed to help me all stacked like bricks on my chest.

I didn't have some grand vision or perfect plan, but I had one thing left: movement. I kept going. I didn't sprint. I didn't soar. I crawled, limped, stumbled, and dragged myself through those years. Through the anger, sadness, and numbness, I just kept moving forward.

Emotional and Social Challenges

The weight of those years seeped into every part of who I was. It shaped how I thought, how I moved through the world, and how I saw myself.

Being labeled as "less than" again and again doesn't just sting in the moment. It rewires your self-worth. It creeps in slowly, telling you you're a burden, that you'll never measure up, that you're the one who always needs extra help, the one who slows everyone down. It tells you, without needing to say it outright, that you'll never be more than the label taped to your file folder.

And let's be clear: these weren't random insults shouted in moments of stress. These were carefully spoken truths, or so they believed, delivered by teachers and JROTC instructors who saw no future for kids like me. Their tone wasn't even always cruel. Sometimes it was worse, disappointed. Resigned. Like I had let them down by not fitting into their mold.

And I absorbed it. All of it.

I learned how to shrink myself in public, to avoid eye contact when teachers handed back assignments, to fake my way through group projects, to laugh things off before anyone could mock me first. I became a master of preemptive self-deprecation, of staying just invisible enough to dodge the full weight of people's assumptions. But inside, I was screaming for someone to see me, really see me. I wanted someone to look past all that and see the fire still burning under the ashes.

There were a few people who did, just enough to keep me going. Friends who showed up. Fellow misfits who stood shoulder to shoulder with me. A couple of teachers who handed me quiet kindness instead of warnings. They were rare, but unforgettable.

I carried those emotional scars for a long time. Some of them are still there, but they no longer control me. I've learned to own my story, the good, the broken, the defiant, the resilient. And while I wouldn't wish my path on anyone, I also wouldn't erase it because it taught me to fight. It taught me to speak up, to lead with empathy, and to never, ever underestimate someone who's been written off, especially when that someone is me. They were sharp, deliberate weapons:

"You're stupid."

"You're not worth the air you breathe."

"You're a waste of space."

They didn't fade with time. Those voices, the ones that called me worthless, dumb, hopeless, didn't just drift away as I grew older. They lingered. They looped in my mind like a broken record, whispering in moments of doubt, shouting in moments of fear. Even as I worked to build a life far from those classrooms and drill fields, even as I collected degrees, accolades, and titles, their words stalked me like shadows I couldn't outrun.

I'd be in a meeting, making a point, and there it was:

"You'll never be anything but a failure."

I'd open a book and struggle with a line of text, and hear:

"How did you even make it to eighth grade?"

The damage dug deep, beneath my skin, beneath my confidence, embedding itself in the very wiring of who I was becoming. Their words weren't just insults. When you're a kid, especially one who is already unsure of your place in the world, those words don't feel like opinions. They feel like facts. Undeniable truths spoken by adults whose job was to guide you. So, you swallow them. And over time, they become part of you.

Socially, it was suffocating. Being in special education was like wearing a flashing neon sign that screamed different. I could feel it the moment I walked into a classroom, the shift in how people looked at me, the hesitation in their voices, the quiet assumptions. I tried to pretend it didn't matter. I told myself I didn't care. But I did. I cared so much it hurt.

JROTC should've been a refuge, a reset button. But even there, no matter how close I was to my fellow cadets, I couldn't shake the feeling of being on the outside. The instructors made sure of that. I tried harder than anyone, showed up early, stayed late, gave everything I had, but they never let me forget where they thought I belonged. I craved belonging. I ached for it. But no matter what I did, they made it clear: I wasn't part of their world.

That longing, for acceptance, for respect, followed me like a shadow. And in the absence of praise, I built something else: humor. Humor became my armor. A quick joke could change the energy in a room, shift the attention away from my shortcomings, turn embarrassment into entertainment. I could disarm a cruel comment with a sharp punchline before it had the chance to land.

The truth behind every laugh was really a plea.

Please see me. Please think I'm worth something.

No matter how loud the laughter, it never drowned out the question that haunted me: Why wasn't I good enough for them to respect?

Still, amidst all the pain and rejection, the friendships I built in JROTC became my lifelines. We were all a little broken, a little misplaced, and in each other, we found fragments of home. In those fleeting moments, I felt seen. I mattered. I wasn't just "that kid" who the adults mocked. I was part of something. That sense of belonging, brief as it was, helped me hang on.

But the damage stayed. The public humiliation, the constant belittlement, the weight of having to prove myself again and again while dragging their words like chains, didn't just go away. I carried it every single day. It shaped how I moved through the world. It became the fuel behind every paper I wrote, every job I took, every challenge I crushed. It also became the burden that wore me down.

Even when I achieved more than they ever dreamed possible, the whisper never stopped:

Keep going.

Don't let them win.

Their words were meant to break me.

They didn't.

If those years taught me anything, it's this: I will never be that voice for someone else. I will never be the reason someone questions their worth.

Turning Doubt into Determination

In twelfth grade, we sat in that special education classroom, IEP students, all of us, and were told with stunning clarity: Passing the high school proficiency test didn't matter. There was no sugarcoating, no pep talk, no "do your best." Just the flat, practiced delivery of a message wrapped in polite smiles and soft voices: Don't bother trying. We don't expect you to pass.

It wasn't guidance. It was surrender.

They handed us this quiet defeat as though it were fact, an invisible contract we were expected to sign without question. Instead of challenging us, they offered us an attendance diploma. A participation trophy, really. Not for learning. Not for earning. Just for showing up. Just for surviving long enough to graduate on paper.

But I wasn't ready to sign that contract. I wasn't okay with that being my ending. I didn't fight through years of humiliation and dismissal to walk across that stage with a diploma that screamed, "We never believed in you." So, I decided to try. Not because I had some bold sense of confidence, I didn't. But because somewhere deep inside, beneath the fear and the self-doubt, something whispered: Prove them wrong.

And I did. I passed.

I passed the test they told me not to bother taking. I did the thing they assumed I couldn't do. And when the results came in, I looked up to see wide eyes and stunned silence. My special education teachers looked at me like I had just pulled off a magic trick. There were no hugs, no high-fives, just disbelief. And disbelief doesn't feel like a compliment when it's pointed at you.

In that moment, I realized just how little they had ever expected from me. And worse, just how shocked they were that I had proved them wrong. What does it say to a kid when the adults meant to guide you are surprised, genuinely stunned, that you succeeded? First, they say, "You can't do it." And then, when you do, they say, 'Wow, I can't believe you actually did."

That's not pride. That's pity in disguise, and it stung more than any failure ever could.

That moment wasn't rare. All through high school, the pattern played on repeat. A broken record of low expectations, masked in "realism." Counselors, teachers, and administrators carried around this unspoken rulebook titled: *How to Lower the Bar Without Anyone Noticing.* It didn't always come as direct insults. Sometimes it came with a smile.

They probably thought they were helping. They weren't. Those words weren't harmless. They were heavy. And the worst part was that kids believed them. I watched classmates, bright, funny, talented kids, stop trying. Not because they weren't capable, but because they trusted the adults who told them they weren't.

They gave up before they even got the chance to see what they could do.

But every time someone told me I couldn't, I tucked it away. I turned it into fuel. Passing that test wasn't just about a diploma. It was me standing up, arms raised, fists clenched, and shouting into the void:

You were wrong about me.

I learned from that experience that you don't have to accept someone else's vision for your life. You don't have to let their doubt define your story. Don't settle. Don't lower the bar to make someone else comfortable. Fight. Fight to become the best version of yourself. Prove them wrong by doing.

As high school finally drew to a close, I was a cocktail of emotions, some expected others confusing. I was angry. Angry at the system, at the teachers who gave up on me, at the instructors who saw me as a problem instead of a person.

But under the anger was something else. Relief. Even hope. I was happy to be leaving. Happy to step away from a place that had misjudged me at every turn. And under the frustration and fatigue, I believed the next step might be different. College wasn't just a transition; it was a shot at a clean slate. A chance to rewrite everything.

I didn't know it then, but everything I endured was already shaping how I'd show up for others.

Chapter 5

Finding Belonging in a Neurotypical World

When I was growing up, my family was my anchor, solid, imperfect, but always there. My parents loved me in their own ways, though they didn't fully grasp the storm I was navigating inside. Dyslexia and ADHD shaped every corner of my life, but from the outside, it was hard to see. My mother, was my fiercest advocate back then, constantly locking horns with the school system, demanding IEP meetings, battling for my spot in special education. She fought for me with a kind of desperation that, as a kid, embarrassed me, but now, as an adult, humbles me.

My mother hung posters all over the walls of our house:

"You are great," "You are smart," "You are capable"

At the time, I rolled my eyes so hard I'm surprised they didn't get stuck. I didn't get it. Why cover the living room walls with what felt like a motivational poster explosion? It was like walking into a Hallmark card factory that had sneezed. But now? Now I see it. She was trying to shield me from the outside voices, the ones saying I was dumb, lazy, not enough. She couldn't protect me from the world, so she did what any mom armed with a printer and a glue stick would do: she built armor out of love… and laminated paper.

She didn't know exactly what I was going through, no parent gets a handbook titled, *How to Raise a Kid Who Hates Spelling Tests and Authority Figures,* but she knew I was struggling. And in her own scrappy, glitter-glued way, she tried to remind me that I mattered. And honestly? Looking back, I think the "You Can Do Hard Things" poster may have saved me more times than I want to admit. Even if it *was* right next to a clipart kitten hanging from a tree branch saying, "Hang in there!"

My father, a quiet man of his generation, was the backbone of our home. Steady, reliable, always working. He didn't step into the school battles, didn't ask many questions about my grades or IEP paperwork. But he was there physically, emotionally distant but solid. He did what he knew: he provided.

What follows is hard to write, hard to read, and even harder to relive.

But everything changed in January of 1987.

That was the month our family shattered.

It happened in the middle of tenth grade in late January, during what should have been just another ordinary week. My older brother, Robby, was working a part-time cleaning job with a subcontractor for General Telephone and Electric (GTE) plant in Henderson, Nevada. He was seventeen, trying to earn money to pay for car insurance. He went to work one evening and never came home. I can still remember that night as if it had just happened:

The phone rang. I picked it up, expecting a friend or maybe someone from school. Instead, a stranger's voice said, "This is St. Rose Hospital. We need to speak to Robert Sims. His son has been brought to the hospital."

I froze. My stomach dropped.

I ran to get my father. I watched his face drain of color as he heard the words no parent should ever hear:

"Your son has been brought in DOA, dead on arrival. You need to come immediately."

We all rushed into the Ford Ranger. No one spoke. We just drove, fast and panicked, toward a reality none of us were ready for.

When we got there, what we found wasn't life. It was a body hooked to machines. My brother's chest rose and fell only because the ventilator forced it to. His arms were strapped down. His face was still. There was no Robby behind his eyes, just a shell held together by wires and a family's desperate hope. Ten days passed. Ten long, gut-wrenching days in the ICU. Ten days of prayers, bargaining, tears. And then, the machines were turned off. The last breath was artificial. The silence afterward was not.

The drive home was unbearable. My dad gripped the wheel like he could squeeze the nightmare out of existence. My mom stared ahead, lost. I sat in the middle, surrounded by the kind of silence that screams. The world outside moved as if nothing had happened. But inside that truck, everything had.

I remember everything. The lights in the ICU. The sterile smell. The beeping of the heart monitor that suddenly wasn't there anymore. The way his skin looked. The weight of knowing he was gone, really gone.

That grief doesn't just pass. It becomes part of you. It settles into your bones.

Robby was more than a brother. He was the steady force I leaned on. Without him, our home became a cracked foundation. My mother buried her grief in fury. She threw herself into a battle with GTE, demanding answers, trying to make someone, anyone, accountable for the accident. My father receded. He worked six days a week and came home to sit silently in his recliner, staring through the television. Even when he was home, he was somewhere else. That silence never lifted. He stayed that way until he passed in 2004.

For months after Robby's death, life still felt like walking through a dream I couldn't wake up from. I have blank spots in my memory from that time, days, maybe weeks, that are just gone. His room stayed the same, frozen in time, both a monument and a wound. We didn't speak much of him. The grief in our house was too loud to name.

I was still just a kid. I needed something, someone, to help make sense of the chaos. But my parents were lost in their own grief, unreachable. So, I turned to my friends. They became my escape, my lifeline. We played pranks, roamed the neighborhood, and filled our lives with laughter. I wasn't carefree, of course, but I was trying to remember what it felt like to be alive. I didn't tell my friends how much I was hurting. I didn't have to. Just being around them helped me breathe.

People say time heals. It doesn't. It just teaches you how to carry the pain better. The scar doesn't fade. It just stops bleeding. And sometimes, even now, it reopens. A song, a smell, a quiet moment—and it all comes rushing back.

Losing my brother changed everything. It made the world feel fragile and sharp. But in the wreckage, I found the beginnings of resilience. I learned that grief doesn't go away. It walks beside you. You just learn how to walk anyway.

And in those moments when the pain feels fresh again, I remind myself that Robby would want me to keep going. To live a life that honors the love we shared. To find purpose in the heartbreak. To tell this story, not for sympathy, but for understanding. Because behind every quiet, struggling kid is a story. And sometimes, telling it is the only way to keep going.

More Than I Could Carry

Being a kid with dyslexia and ADHD already felt like trying to run a marathon with my shoelaces tied together. Every day was a struggle to keep up, to stay focused, to decode a world that didn't seem built for someone like me. But nothing, nothing, prepared me for what came next.

When my brother died, everything I thought was hard became almost unbearable.

It wasn't just the grief; it was the shock that rewired my entire existence. One moment, I was trying to stay afloat in school, misunderstood and mislabeled. The next, I was standing in an ICU, staring at the lifeless body of the one person who made me feel like I wasn't alone. Robby wasn't just my brother, he was my compass, my anchor. And in one tragic moment, I lost him.

Suddenly, the struggle to read, to focus, to behave, didn't matter anymore. Not because it wasn't hard, it was still brutally hard, but because now I was also carrying the kind of pain no kid should ever have to carry. My world was turned upside down, and the fragile tools I'd been slowly building to manage my learning differences felt completely useless against the avalanche of grief.

Teachers didn't know what to do with me. Friends didn't know what to say. No one did. And I don't blame them; this kind of loss leaves everyone speechless. But it complicated everything. Because I wasn't just the kid who couldn't sit still, who couldn't spell, who always seemed "off." Now I was the kid who had lost his brother. The kid with sadness spilling out of his pores and no words to explain it.

I acted out.

I became louder, more disruptive, more unpredictable. Not because I wanted attention, but because I didn't know how to ask for help. I didn't have the language to describe what grief felt like, so I let my behavior speak for me. I hid my pain behind laughter, defiance, and sarcasm. It was easier to be "the bad kid" than the broken one.

Grieving with ADHD is like trying to catch the wind while drowning. You feel everything all at once, but it's scattered, messy, and relentless. I couldn't concentrate, couldn't sleep, couldn't explain the heaviness inside of me. And dyslexia made it even harder to process any of it. I couldn't write down what I felt. I couldn't read books that may have helped. All I could do was feel, and even that felt too big to carry.

There were moments, long moments, when I thought about not going on at all. And that pain didn't pass quickly. It lingered for years. It lived in my chest like a shadow I couldn't shake. I never said it out loud, never told my parents, my teachers, or even my closest friends. But suicide crept into my thoughts more than once, quietly, dangerously. I masked it behind jokes and rebellion, but the truth is, I didn't want to hurt, I just wanted the hurt to stop. Even today, the pain is still there, but now I can navigate it without such thoughts.

If it wasn't for a few close friends, real ones, the kind who don't need words to understand you, I don't think I would have made it. They were my escape, my oxygen.

Everything became heavier. School felt irrelevant. Home felt broken.

I didn't know how to be a kid anymore.

That loss didn't just complicate my challenges, it multiplied them. It layered trauma over confusion, grief over frustration, silence over noise. And somehow, I had to keep moving. I kept pretending I was okay. I kept showing up in a world that now felt impossibly dark.

But that's the thing about surviving as a neurodivergent kid in grief, you learn how to adapt in ways no one sees. You learn how to find the cracks of light in the darkness. And slowly, quietly, you begin to rebuild.

Relationships with Siblings and Friends

Growing up, my brother and I were classic siblings, or at least, our own chaotic version of it. Just twenty months apart, we fought like MMA fighters trapped in an endless championship match. There were no rounds, no referees, just two stubborn boys throwing fists, elbows, and the occasional toy truck across the living room. Sometimes he'd win. Sometimes I'd win. And more often than not, it ended in blood, usually ours, and a broom-wielding mother yelling, "You're going to kill each other!"

Spoiler alert: We didn't. Though honestly, there were moments it felt like we might.

To someone outside the madness, say, my wife, this didn't seem like a typical sibling relationship. She cringes every time I tell her about one of our more intense "battles," eyes wide in disbelief. "That is not classic," she always says. "That is not normal." But what does she know? She has a brother. Singular. That's not the same. She never had the full-contact, emotionally confusing experience of having a brother so close in age that your identities sometimes bled together… right before your knuckles did.

The truth is, for two strong-willed boys in the 1980s, rough housing wasn't dysfunction, it was communication. It was competition, sure, but also connection. We tested limits constantly, our own and each other's. We were stubborn, fiercely independent, always trying to prove something. But beneath the bruises and brawls was something deeper: respect. Loyalty. That unspoken brotherly language where you could scream at each other one minute and defend each other the next without missing a beat.

We were a strange breed of best frenemies. We could be throwing punches in the hallway at 3:00 p.m. and covering for each other when the neighbors came knocking at 3:15. If someone else tried to mess with one of us, at school, in the neighborhood, anywhere, we instantly teamed up like an amateur version of the Avengers. All our battles were forgotten in a heartbeat when the threat came from outside our bloodline.

The same rules applied to our neighborhood crew. We fought amongst ourselves like it was a rite of passage, every scraped knee and chipped tooth was its own badge of honor. But let some kid from another block wander over with an attitude, and suddenly we were one unit. Unified. Loyal. We might have tried to knock each other's teeth out on Monday, but by Tuesday, we were side-by-side defending our turf like it was sacred ground.

Looking back, it's almost funny in that bittersweet kind of way. The chaos, the noise, the broken lamps and broom handles, it all painted a picture of two boys who didn't know how to express their bond any way other than full contact. But it was loyalty, through and through. We might have been loud, reckless, and a little unhinged, but underneath all that was a kind of love that didn't need words. It was shown in the way we stood up for each other, even when we were covered in bruises from our last fight.

And then, just as things were beginning to shift, as we were stepping into that next chapter where the anger was fading and the bond was evolving, he was gone.

We were finally getting past the fists and the fire. We were growing up. Maturing. Learning that not every disagreement needed to end with a headlock or a dented wall. We were starting to laugh more than we shouted, to talk instead of fight. We were on the edge of becoming not just brothers, but friends.

He never got to make that full transition.

That's the part that stays with me. The almost. The just-about-to-be. All the moments we never got to live because life, in one cruel instant, stole the future we were just beginning to build. And now, every memory, every ridiculous, loud, bloody, hilarious memory, is tinged with the ache of knowing we didn't get to finish writing our story together.

And yet, those memories are a gift. Because in all that noise, all that chaos, all those wild days of childhood, he showed me what it means to have someone in your corner, even when you're the one who just punched them in the jaw five minutes earlier.

That was us. Two brothers. A little broken, a lot bonded. And for a while, it was the best team I ever had.

My Sister: A World Apart

I also have a sister who is about six years older than I am. When you're young, that age gap may as well be a hundred years. She was in a completely different world, hanging out with her friends, married, and living a life I couldn't begin to understand. While I was tangled in sibling brawls and chaotic boyhood antics, she was in her own world, a married world, with kids, a husband, and her own responsibilities. We were worlds apart.

Being the youngest, I was light years away from her in terms of age and interests. Honestly, I'm sure my brother and I, with our constant MMA-style battles and general chaos, were more annoying than anything to her. She kept her distance, and I don't blame her. We were just two unruly boys constantly fighting over the TV or whatever nonsense brothers find important.

Our lives rarely overlapped back then. I was still just a kid, while she was building her own life, and at the time, I didn't really understand that. To me, she was just...gone. Not in an intentional way, but in the way that happens when life moves at different speeds for different people.

Friendships: A Lifeline

During those years, my friends became more than just people to hang out with, they became my lifeline. They didn't know what I was carrying. How could they? They couldn't see the shame, the chaos, the pressure building up inside me like a shaken soda ready to blow. But being with them gave me something I couldn't find anywhere else: relief. A few precious hours where I could breathe, where the pressure of home, school, and the silent grief that blanketed everything could take a backseat.

Instead of drowning in stress, I played the role of the class-clown with a PhD in sarcasm. I cracked jokes, dropped quick comebacks, and found ways to get a laugh even when I was failing. Couldn't ace the spelling test? No problem, make the whole class laugh until they forgot I even took it. Humor became my smoke screen. Crack a joke, dodge the pity. Keep it light, keep it funny, and maybe no one will notice I'm falling apart. It was like I became the director, the writer, and the lead actor in my own sitcom. On the outside, I looked like I had it together. Inside? I was only crying during the commercial breaks.

Friendships were more than social connections, they were air. After school hangouts, driving around town with the windows down, or sitting on someone's front porch talking about absolutely nothing... those moments were everything. Those were the only times the noise faded, when I didn't have to wear the weight of grief, anxiety, and failure. My friends didn't have to say the right thing. They didn't even need to understand. Just being there was enough. Their presence gave me something rare: a moment when I wasn't drowning.

The Wide-Reaching Impact of Dyslexia and ADHD

Most people think dyslexia and ADHD just show up in the classroom, wrong. These weren't just academic challenges; they spilled into every corner of my life. They shaped my social world, my self-esteem, my relationships, everything. Even now, as an adult, there are days when they still sneak in through the back door and throw a wrench into something I thought I had figured out.

Friendships and relationships took the same hits as my schoolwork

Dyslexia made communication difficult. Sometimes the words just didn't come out right, I'd twist a sentence until it lost its meaning or blurt something that didn't land the way I intended. Other times, I'd misread what someone was saying entirely and respond like I was in a completely different conversation. I couldn't keep up in fast-talking groups, missing punchlines, reacting too slowly, or laughing when everyone else had moved on. I was always one beat behind, stuck trying to play catch-up in a game I didn't fully understand.

ADHD didn't help. I had a brain that didn't believe in brakes. I forgot things. I interrupted. I jumped topics mid-sentence. I got distracted mid-story and never came back to it. My hyperactivity made me the life of the party one moment and "too much" the next. A friend once told me being around me was like trying to drink from a firehose— you'd either drown or laugh your way through it.

My impulsiveness? That's where things got wild. Like the time I threw a lit match into the hair of a neighborhood friend, thinking it would be funny, and watched in horror as his hair actually caught fire. Or when I knocked on the door of a grumpy old man, called him a few choice names I'd picked up from cartoons or older kids, then ran like hell back to my house, while he watched exactly where I went. Or the masterpiece: when I somehow got ahold of some gunpowder, built a massive firecracker with a fuse, and lit it in the garage while my next-door friend's mom and her friends were chatting inside.

BAM. What a noise.

What a disaster.

And of course… what a visit to my parents, who were way past tired of the chaos I dragged home with me.

I wasn't trying to be reckless; I just didn't stop to think through the consequences of my actions. Instead, I acted and felt the consequences later. The fallout always came, sometimes in the form of angry parents (and teachers), sometimes with singed eyebrows, and sometimes in the silent drift of a friend who wasn't sure if I was safe to be around anymore.

Eventually, those impulsive stunts started to stick to me. I wasn't just "Doug, the hyper kid" anymore; I became "the troublemaker." The kid parents warned their kids about. The neighborhood "hoodlum." The kid people crossed the street to avoid because I was unpredictable. And once that label stuck, it was hard to shake. Every mistake I made just seemed to confirm what people already believed. I wasn't just misunderstood; I was branded.

In public school, friendships are often born in the classroom, group projects, casual conversations, lunch tables. But I was placed in self-contained special education classes, isolated from most of my peers. My classmates had struggles of their own, many of them navigating lives even harder than mine. Connections didn't come easy in those rooms, and honestly, I didn't even know how to make them. I felt different, awkward, and misunderstood, because I was. I didn't fit into their world, and I sure didn't fit into the mainstream.

So, I doubled down on what worked: Humor. Energy. Noise. If I couldn't impress anyone with my grades, I'd win them over with laughs. I became the one who always had a joke ready, the one who kept things light. It wasn't just about being funny. It was about survival. Being the class clown was how I stayed visible in a world that kept trying to forget I was there.

But humor couldn't fix everything. ADHD made holding onto friendships hard. I'd forget to call people back. I'd lose track of conversations. I'd interrupt and jump from topic to topic like a pinball, struggling to notice when someone needed me to listen or just be still. I often didn't know when I was being too much. I didn't realize when someone was pulling away. And even when I did, I didn't know how to fix it.

Relationships got even trickier as I got older. ADHD made my emotions intense and unpredictable. I could be deeply engaged one moment and miles away the next. Reading social situations was also hard. I'd misread things, not read things fully, forget details, and struggle to put my thoughts into words. The result? Misunderstandings. Frustration. Distance. Not because I didn't care, but because everything that came so easily to others felt like a puzzle I was constantly trying to solve.

Over time, I learned. I started to notice when I was spiraling, when my impulsiveness was driving someone away, or when my attention had drifted too far. I practiced listening, really listening, and trained myself to pause before jumping into a conversation. I picked up strategies to keep myself on track: sticky notes, alarms, reminders on my phone. I stopped pretending I didn't struggle and started finding ways to work around it.

Even today, social interactions require more effort because dyslexia and ADHD don't go away. Sometimes I interrupt too much. I may forget something important someone told me or zone out in the middle of a conversation and come back wondering what I missed. Sometimes, I walk away from my family in the middle of a conversation because I suddenly think of something I have to do and don't want to forget (spoiler: this doesn't go over well). It's not intentional. It's just part of how I'm wired.

I used to think these things made me broken. Now, I see them for what they really are: part of my blueprint. Flawed, sure. Complicated, definitely. But also filled with a kind of strength that doesn't always look like strength on the outside. A strength built not on ease, but on effort.

And I'm still learning. Still adjusting. Still fighting to hold onto the connections that matter most. But I know this now, I'm not alone in that fight. And if you're in it too, I promise, neither are you.

Using Pain as Fuel

I carried the pain of my childhood into adulthood. And with that pain came a relentless drive to prove everyone wrong. And I did prove them wrong. But it also came at an emotional cost.

I didn't know how to stop. I didn't know how to rest. I didn't know how to feel proud, because the minute I hit one goal, the voices came rushing back, daring me to hit the next. It was like I believed that success could erase the pain. That if I pushed hard enough, long enough, I'd wake up one day free from the scars.

But it doesn't work that way.

Even now, having achieved things I once thought impossible, including earning advanced degrees, leadership roles, and recognition as an expert in my field, I still hear those voices whisper. I still wake up some mornings wondering if I've done enough, if I've earned my place, if maybe, just maybe, they were right all along.

That's the thing about trauma born from words: it doesn't fade easily. It digs in. It weaves itself into the way you see the world, and yourself.

But I didn't do this alone. I found strength in people who saw past the struggle. The friendships I forged during those chaotic years, the few mentors who reached into the darkness and said, "I see you," the friends who stuck around even when I was messy and sarcastic and angry at the world, they were everything. They didn't need me to prove anything. Their belief in me gave me permission to be something more than a walking rebuttal to everyone who ever doubted me.

They were my lifeline. My reset button. My mirror when I couldn't see anything in myself worth believing in.

And it was through them, and the journey it took to find them, that I learned what kind of person I wanted to be.

I made a promise to myself, one I carry with me into every classroom, every boardroom, every conversation with a struggling student or frustrated peer: I will never be the kind of leader who tears people down.

I know what that feels like. I know how deep the damage goes. I know how long it takes to crawl out from under that kind of shame. So instead, I choose to build. To believe. To help others see what they're capable of, even if all they've ever been told is that they'll never measure up.

In many ways, my past became a blueprint for my future.

I learned resilience from the worst moments of my life.

I learned compassion from surviving cruelty.

I learned humor as a shield, and then as a bridge.

And I learned that the words we speak to others can either wound them for life… or help them heal.

The scars are still there. I feel them sometimes when I'm alone with my thoughts, when something triggers an old memory, when doubt creeps in late at night. But I don't hide from them anymore. I let them remind me, not of the pain, but of the journey.

I am not dumb.

I am not a broken kid in the back of a special ed class.

I never was.

My story is proof that they were wrong.

Chapter 6

Surviving College with Dyslexia and Drive

Walking onto the campus at UNLV for the first time in the fall of 1989, I felt something I hadn't felt in a long time: hope. Maybe, just maybe, college would be my fresh start. A new chapter. A clean slate. After years of being underestimated, mislabeled, and shuffled through the public school system like expired lunch meat, I told myself this was my chance to prove I actually belonged in a place of learning. You know, the kind with books, syllabi, and vending machines that sometimes worked.

But that hope didn't last long.

My first two years of college were some of the hardest, most demoralizing years of my life. It felt like I was trying to climb a jagged mountain with no gear, no map, and a backpack filled with bowling balls and bad advice. Only instead of rocks and snow, I was scaling years of educational neglect, deeply rooted self-doubt, and an ongoing WWE-style smackdown with my dyslexia and ADHD.

From Day One, I was already flirting with dropping out. The academic leap from high school to college didn't feel like a step, it felt like being launched out of a cannon into a course catalog I couldn't decipher. My high school diploma? Let's just say it was less "evidence of preparedness" and more "congrats, you survived!" There had been no crash course in critical thinking, no deep dive into structuring essays, and definitely no "How to Take Notes Without Having a Full-On Panic Attack" elective.

While other students strolled into lectures like they'd been training for this since birth, I was in the back of the room trying to decode the syllabus like it was written in ancient Sanskrit. Every assignment felt like a cruel game of "How Dumb Can We Make You Feel Today?" I couldn't structure a sentence, at least, not one that didn't read like a Mad Lib. I'd read the same passage five times and still feel like it had been written by a drunk philosopher.

My ADHD made it impossible to sit through a full lecture without mentally redecorating the room, replaying old conversations, or wondering if squirrels ever get bored. My dyslexia made every reading assignment feel like running a marathon in flip-flops, slow, painful, and deeply unflattering. While my classmates confidently asked questions and submitted polished work, I was in the academic equivalent of a doggy paddle, just trying not to sink.

For years, I'd hidden my dyslexia like a state secret. But in college, hiding it became like trying to sneak an elephant through a revolving door. Professors didn't have time for struggling students, and they made that clear without blinking. Many didn't just misunderstand learning differences; they seemed genuinely annoyed that we existed. Their disdain wasn't subtle either. You could hear it in their tone, see it in their eyerolls, and feel it in the way they said, "Well, that's your responsibility," like they were allergic to empathy.

Some outright refused to accommodate me. I was labeled quickly: "average" if they were feeling generous, "lazy" if they hadn't had their coffee.

Turns out, college didn't come with a clean slate.

But what it did come with was a whole new set of battles, and I was just getting started.

It felt like high school all over again.

The old voices returned, whispering in the back of my mind, echoing louder with each failure:

"You're not college material."

"You should be sweeping floors or working in a warehouse, not sitting in a university lecture hall."

And some days... I believed them.

Some days, I looked around and thought maybe they were right. Maybe I was kidding myself. Maybe this world wasn't meant for people like me, kids who couldn't spell, who couldn't stay focused, who couldn't keep up. I felt alone, defeated, and humiliated. I came close, so close, to walking away. But for reasons I didn't fully understand at the time, I stayed.

I didn't stay because I was strong. I stayed because I was angry. Because I was tired of being told who I was and what I couldn't do..

This chapter of my life isn't just about the failure. It's about what came next. It's about the small wins, the paper I finally managed to write without tears, the professor who didn't look through me, the classmate who treated me like I wasn't broken. It's about the slow, painful process of finding my footing, even when the ground kept shifting beneath me.

I didn't thrive in those first few years. I survived them. One class. One assignment. One long night at a time. And while the scars of those days are still with me, so are the lessons. That's how I started to move forward, not with giant leaps, but with quiet defiance and the determination to not be dismissed again.

Significant Struggles and Small Victories

I wasn't remotely prepared, academically, emotionally, or mentally, for the leap from high school to college. And how could I have been? The voices of my past were still clanging in my head like a broken bell tower: "You'll never get into UNLV, let alone pass, succeed, or graduate. You should look into trade school." Those words weren't just careless remarks, they were curses, ones I carried like a second skin. I tried to shake them off, but they followed me, echoed in every lecture, every classroom, every assignment.

Before long, the F's and D's started stacking up like parking tickets on a car. Each failed assignment felt like a fresh paper cut to the soul. Another little reminder that maybe my high school teachers had been right. Maybe I was wasting everyone's time, including mine. It had a certain tragic poetry to it, like the world's worst Hallmark movie:

"The Boy They Said Would Never Make It... Didn't."

Spoiler alert: I flunked out of college not once, but twice in those early years. And each time, it hit like a gut punch I never saw coming, even though, in hindsight, the warning signs were flashing brighter than a Vegas marquee.

The worst part wasn't just the failing. It was failing while trying. Really trying. Like giving-it-everything-you've-got, highlighting-textbooks-you-don't-understand kind of trying. Showing up early. Staying late. Asking questions that got met with glazed eyes and audible sighs. The kind of trying that should've earned me a sticker or at least a mildly encouraging nod. But nope. Just another reminder that effort doesn't always equal outcome.

And then came the indifference. Honestly, that may have stung even worse than the F's. Some professors couldn't even remember my name, despite the fact that I was the guy who sat in the front row blinking in panic like a deer in a Scantron factory. I'd ask a question and get a sigh so loud it probably registered on the Richter scale. Some would glance at my paper like I'd just handed them a receipt for emotional damage.

My dyslexia and ADHD weren't seen as challenges to support, they were treated like proof that I didn't belong in higher education at all. It was high school déjà vu, only now with more tuition and less mercy.

Still, I had a spark. And when things got unbearable, I used it. Every dismissal, every eye-roll, every sarcastic comment about my intelligence, it fueled me. I refused to let them win. I refused to give them the satisfaction of being right.

In a strange, twisted way, their disbelief became my drive.

But I didn't do it alone.

At my lowest, when I was failing classes and fighting every demon in my head, there was one person who didn't see a waste of space, my girlfriend (now wife). She saw potential. She never once said, "You can't." She never let me quit. Her belief in me wasn't loud or flashy, it was quiet and steady, like a lighthouse cutting through fog. She saw that my failures weren't from laziness or lack of intelligence. They were the scars of an education system that had let me down at every turn.

She took the time to teach me what others had never bothered to. How to structure a paper. How to organize my thoughts. How to break assignments in manageable pieces. Her support was the academic scaffolding I never had. But more than that, she gave me the one thing I needed more than anything else: the belief that I could do it.

Her faith helped me return to UNLV. Helped me finish my bachelor's degree. And eventually, it helped me stand in front of my own students at the College of Southern Nevada, not as someone who had all the answers, but as someone who understood the fight.

And that's why I teach the way I do. That's why I go out of my way to lift up the students who are drowning, the ones nobody else sees. I know their fight. I know what it's like to be told you're not enough, that you don't belong. And I know the power of just one person who says, I see you. I believe in you. Keep going.

I was never a waste of space. Never a lost cause. And I will spend the rest of my life making sure no student ever feels that way on my watch.

Developing Coping Strategies and Finding Mentors

It wasn't until my second academic suspension, my first real sabbatical, that something shifted. I didn't plan for it to be meaningful. Honestly, it felt more like a consequence than an opportunity. But during that forced year off, something unexpected happened: I got a real job. Not a side gig or something to just pass the time, but my first professional job. And in that space, for the first time, I was surrounded by other people who didn't see me as broken.

They valued education, sure, but more importantly, they valued potential. They looked at my work ethic, my willingness to learn, and my determination to show up and contribute. And they told me something I hadn't heard in a long time, maybe ever. They said, "You should go back to school. You have more in you than this."

That year wasn't just about earning a paycheck; it became a crash course in figuring out who I was and, more importantly, who I didn't want to become. Working unskilled, dead-end jobs, clocking in and out with sore feet and sore pride, it sucked. The physical grind was tough, but the emotional grind was worse. I saw what life could look like if I stayed on that path: limited, exhausting, and hollow. And that terrified me more than any test ever had.

But that job also brought me something else: belief. Real belief, from people who had no reason to give it. They didn't care about my GPA or that I'd flunked out of college twice. They cared about what I could do. They saw more in me than I had seen in myself in a long, long time. "Don't stop at the BA," they said. "Go for the whole ball of wax." And that simple line stuck with me. It planted a seed I didn't even know I could nurture. Maybe… just maybe… I could go further than anyone ever thought I would.

That year off wasn't just a break, it was a turning point. The place where shame slowly turned into vision. Where failure turned into clarity. I realized that if I really wanted a life that meant something to me, I couldn't just drift anymore. I had to fight for it.

When I made the decision to go back to UNLV, I wasn't alone. My then-girlfriend stood by me like a rock. While professors and systems had let me down, she never did. She didn't just support me emotionally; she quite literally taught me how to survive college. The broken public school system hadn't equipped me with the most basic academic tools. I had never been shown how to study effectively, how to take notes, how to organize my thoughts into coherent writing.

She became my guide. My tutor. My lifeline. She taught me how to take notes, how to outline a paper, how to study without burning out. She showed me how to approach assignments one step at a time. Where others saw a lost cause, she saw potential. Where I saw gaps, she built bridges.

And writing, God, writing was the hardest. Still is. With dyslexia, words don't line up the way they should. Sentences lose their meaning halfway through. Spelling is a battlefield. Paragraphs collapse into chaos. You don't outgrow that. You just learn to live with it, to find workarounds, to build structure where your brain wants to go freeform. She sat with me, patiently, and helped me build that structure, one painful piece at a time.

I also tried to get help from the university itself, but back then most universities didn't offer the kind of support for students with learning differences that many have today. Their services were very limited; they didn't offer anything that fit the unique challenges of students with dyslexia or ADHD. There was no roadmap, no tailored support, no real understanding of how these conditions affect someone trying to navigate higher education.

So, I built my own support system.

I found mentors outside the classroom, people who didn't need me to fit into a mold. I leaned hard on my wife, who kept believing in me even when I couldn't. And I started developing coping strategies that worked for me, strategies born not from academic theory, but from sheer necessity.

That was when everything began to shift. Slowly. Painfully. But undeniably.

That year off taught me that failure doesn't have to be final. That the people who dismiss you don't get the last word. That there is always a way forward, even if you have to dig it out yourself with your bare hands.

And most importantly, I learned that you don't have to be perfect to be worthy. You just have to be willing to keep going.

The Ongoing Struggle with Writing

Even today, writing remains one of the hardest things I do. It's not just a task, it's a test. Every time I sit down to write, it feels like climbing a steep, jagged hill. The slope never gets easier, even though I've climbed it a thousand times. It takes persistence, focus, and an uncomfortable amount of self-reflection. I can't just throw words on the page and walk away. I have to wrestle with them. Rearranging, refining, rereading. Over and over again.

It doesn't come naturally. It never has. For me, writing is slow, deliberate, and full of second-guessing. I'll look at a sentence and wonder if it makes sense, if the spelling is right, if the structure holds. I'll rewrite a paragraph five times before it feels close to right. Then I'll rewrite it again.

But I'm not alone in it, and that's made all the difference.

My wife, who happens to be an incredible writer, has been my anchor in the storm. Since the beginning, she's looked over my work, not just as an editor, but as someone who truly believes in me. She catches the misspellings, the awkward phrases, the moments where my brain skipped ahead of my fingers. She polishes my rough ideas and helps me find the confidence to share what I've written.

She sees the potential in my voice even when I can't.

If it weren't for her, I honestly don't know if I would have made it through college. I don't say that lightly. The frustration I felt in those early years, the embarrassment, the overwhelming sense that I didn't belong, nearly broke me. I spent so many nights staring at a blank screen, panicked, paralyzed by the fear that I'd never get the words out right. I questioned myself constantly. Do I really deserve to be here? Am I just fooling myself?

But she refused to let me give up.

She never allowed me to buy into the lie that I wasn't capable. She sat with me when the words wouldn't come. She reminded me that struggle doesn't mean failure. She believed in the man behind the dyslexia, behind the missed commas and backwards letters. And slowly, because of her, I started to believe in that man too.

What I've come to understand is that writing, real writing, isn't about being perfect. It's about showing up again, and again. It's about persistence. And courage. It's about the willingness to try, to revise, to be vulnerable, and to get better over time.

I don't write effortlessly. I probably never will. But I write with heart. I write with intention. And I write with the understanding that every word is a step forward, no matter how steep the path feels.

Today, writing still scares me. But I don't let that fear stop me anymore. I treat it the way I've treated every challenge in my life: with resilience, with grit, and with the humility to lean on the people who love me, especially the one who's been in my corner from the very beginning.

I may never write like her. But I've found my own voice. And that, for me, is everything.

Earning My Bachelor's Degree

This time, I did it differently. I didn't just stumble through, this time, I learned from my failures. And believe it or not, failure became one of my greatest teachers. Looking back now, I realize that the people who never fall, never grow. They never stretch beyond what's easy or safe. Me? I've tripped, tumbled, and face-planted more times than I can count, but I've always gotten back up. That's what moved me forward.

When I returned to UNLV after my second academic suspension, I did so with a strategy. I stopped trying to hide my dyslexia and ADHD and started trying to understand them. I asked for help. I worked slower but smarter. Eventually, I crossed that finish line, earning my bachelor's degree in Anthropology. It took me six years, two longer than it should have, but I didn't care. My final GPA? A 2.73. Again, I didn't care. That degree wasn't about numbers. It wasn't about a piece of paper. It was proof. Proof that I could do it, despite every teacher, every class, every failure, and every dark night where I wanted to walk away.

For the first time, I silenced the voices that had haunted me for so long. For once, I was enough.

Graduate School: A Different Kind of War

Then came graduate school, and holy hell, I thought undergrad was hard.

I walked into that program with a degree in hand, thinking I had finally figured it out. But grad school wasn't just a step up, it was a whole different beast. There was no hiding anymore. No coasting. No "good enough."

Faculty didn't care about my ADHD and dyslexia. They didn't care that I had come from behind or that I worked twice as hard as my peers. They expected perfection. Clarity. Precision. Deadlines met without exception. Ideas articulated like clockwork. I was back at the bottom of the ladder, and this time, the climb was vertical.

Every paper I submitted felt like a minefield. Every exam like a trapdoor waiting to swallow me. I couldn't skim like the others. I couldn't retain information without reading it five times. I couldn't whip up a paper in a weekend and hope for a B. I was still fighting every word, every sentence, every paragraph. My writing, though improved, still felt like dragging thoughts through molasses and trying to make them land with grace.

In grad school, there was no safety net. The competition was fierce. My cohort wasn't just a group of classmates, they were rivals. We were all fighting for research opportunities, for faculty attention, for the right to stay in the game. It was like Survivor, but with APA formatting and thesis deadlines instead of tiki torches and rice.

I was the one everyone thought wouldn't make it. And I knew they thought that. Some pitied me, some respected the hustle, and a few just watched, waiting for me to fall apart. And honestly? I almost did. More than once. But here's the thing: I'd been underestimated my whole life. Now, I was not about to quit.

I had been told I wouldn't make it since elementary school. That I didn't belong. That I wasn't smart enough. And now, here I was, standing toe-to-toe with people who had never had to fight like I had. Maybe they were quicker. Maybe their writing sparkled. But I had something they didn't, I had grit.

And somehow, against all odds, I was the first in my cohort to graduate with my master's degree.

Funny, isn't it? The kid they said wouldn't survive college at all, ended up beating everyone to the finish line.

I've learned that persistence beats talent when talent doesn't have to struggle. In a world where intelligence is treated like currency, my resilience became my greatest asset. I didn't always know the answer. I didn't always get it right the first, or even third, time. But I kept going. Always.

That's what made the difference.

Criticism and Resolve

They didn't sugarcoat anything in graduate school, not the content, not the workload, and definitely not the feedback.

Faculty didn't pull punches when it came to my shortcomings. Professors were blunt, sometimes to the point of brutality. One handed back a paper that looked like it had been murdered in red ink. Scrawled across the top margin, in sharp, impatient handwriting, were the words: "This reads like a rough draft, did you even proofread it?" Another, after I delivered what I thought was a passionate seminar presentation, waited until the classroom cleared before pulling me aside and saying, "You've got the passion, but if you can't articulate your ideas clearly, you're not going to make it in this program."

Constructive? Maybe. Soul-crushing? Absolutely.

Every comment, every side glance, every disapproving tone felt like a not-so-subtle reminder that I didn't belong in their world. That I wasn't built for academia. That they were just waiting for me to burn out and disappear quietly.

And yet, this wasn't my first rodeo with low expectations.

By now, I had built up a tolerance to doubt. I knew how to take their skepticism and turn it into fuel. Their harsh critiques didn't break me. If anything, they sharpened my edge. I didn't collapse under their words; I got to work.

I used their feedback like a map. Every misplaced comma, every vague idea, every awkward transition; I took notes. I made appointments during office hours. I sat down with the same professors who weren't shy about telling me I was falling short. One of them told me bluntly, "You're improving, but don't get comfortable. We're not lowering the bar."

Tough love? Maybe. But I wasn't there for comfort, I was there to finish what I started.

Writing still didn't come naturally. It never has. But I leaned on every tool I'd picked up since undergrad, breaking down assignments into smaller pieces, revising like a madman, and always showing up prepared to fight tooth and nail through another draft. I didn't produce brilliance. But I produced work. Work that, slowly but surely, started to get nods instead of sighs.

And eventually, they noticed.

Crossing the Finish Line

When the day finally came to defend my thesis, it didn't feel like a triumphant march to glory. It felt like stepping into the ring one last time, bloodied but unbowed.

I stood in front of my committee, presenting the culmination of every late night, every revision, every soul-sucking moment of self-doubt I had endured. It wasn't perfect. I knew that. But it was mine. And it was done.

After the presentation, two of the professors on my committee didn't hesitate to keep it real. They looked me in the eye, and one of them said,

"Your thesis is acceptable, but just barely. You should've aimed to be the best."

Ouch.

Maybe they were right. Maybe the writing wasn't groundbreaking. Maybe I didn't walk away with academic glory trailing behind me like a cape. But at that point? I didn't care. I wasn't chasing perfection; I was clawing my way toward completion.

I had poured everything I had into that thesis. I had nothing left to give. Every paragraph had been rewritten a dozen times. Every citation double-checked. Every ounce of willpower had been wrung out and spent. I wasn't the best. But I had made it. And in graduate school, that's everything.

I wasn't the star of the cohort. But I was the first to finish. On time. Which in grad school is the academic equivalent of spotting a unicorn in the wild. Most students in my program took years longer. They dragged through thesis edits, stalled out, disappeared into jobs or burnout.

But not me. I finished. Because I refused to quit.

And in a program where intelligence was currency, and comparison was constant, my greatest asset wasn't raw brainpower, it was relentless, dogged persistence. The kind you forge in the fire of being told your whole life that you'll never make it. I wasn't the fastest. I wasn't the cleanest writer. But I was the most stubborn, and that's what got me across the finish line.

That thesis might have been held together by caffeine, stubbornness, and more late-night breakdowns than I care to admit. But when I turned it in, and it was stamped, approved, and accepted, I felt like I had won my own Olympic event. Because I did.

After everything I'd been through, crossing that finish line felt like winning an Olympic gold medal, if the event was barely surviving grad school and the medal was a thesis held together by sheer willpower and caffeine.

My medal was a master's degree earned not by talent alone, but by grit, sweat, and the refusal to stay down.

And in the end, that's what mattered.

What I gained wasn't just a master's degree. I walked out of that program with something even more valuable: the deep, unshakable belief that hard work wins. That sure beats perfection. And that if you keep swinging, even when you feel like you're down for the count, you can still land a knockout punch.

That lesson prepared me for life.

Breaking Barriers for Students Like Me

I didn't see many students like me in that graduate program. No one with learning differences like dyslexia and ADHD. And not because they couldn't be there, because the system made sure they weren't.

It still weighs heavy on me, not because they don't belong, but because they do. Not because they can't succeed, but because they absolutely can. Yet I know all too well that the path is riddled with invisible barriers, barriers that say, you're not cut out for this. Barriers that don't offer extra time or understanding. That doesn't pause for your processing style. That don't see your potential through your spelling mistakes.

I've seen brilliant minds crushed by those walls. I've watched students who had everything it takes get worn down, not by the subject matter, but by the exhaustion of proving themselves every single day.

It's not right.

I believe, with everything in me, that students with learning differences can and should thrive in graduate programs, but it takes finding the right department, the right mentors, the right space that sees value in diversity of thought, process, and experience. We need to build those spaces. We need to stop pretending perfection is the only ticket to success.

Because if students like me had access to environments that valued persistence over polish, we'd change the world. My journey is proof that the impossible isn't so impossible after all. It's just really, really hard. But not unreachable, and I want more students to reach.

Lessons from My University Days

College handed me both a degree and a mirror, one I had to look into every day and ask, "Can I keep going? "There were so many moments when the answer felt like no. When failure seemed final. When the statements "You'll never make it. You're not smart enough. You should be cleaning tables" came roaring back like ghosts I couldn't exorcise. And yet, I kept showing up. I failed. I tried again. I failed again. I kept showing up.

And somewhere along the line, those failures stopped being the end. They became chapters in a larger story. Chapters about adapting. Working harder. Finding new ways through when the old ones didn't work.

The victories came slower, fewer and farther between, but each one was sweeter than anyone else could understand. Because they were mine. Because they weren't supposed to happen. Because I had to fight for them tooth and nail… and sometimes with coffee, panic, and last-minute prayers to the gods of spellcheck.

Those college years changed me. And no, I didn't become the best student. I did finally realize that being the best student wasn't the goal. Becoming the most stubborn, most determined, most *"You're gonna have to drag me out of here"* student was the secret sauce. That's what saved me. That's what built the life I have now, one painfully earned one B-minus at a time.

The voices from my past haven't vanished. The insults from JROTC instructors, the labels from teachers, the dark whisper of you're not enough, they still show up like uninvited guests at a party I forgot I was throwing. They linger like bad hold music. But they don't get the final word anymore.

I've repurposed them. Upcycled them, really, turned every snide comment and eye roll into motivational kindling. Every person who doubted me added another log to the fire. And instead of burning me out, they lit a blaze I refused to let die. I turned their doubt into my personal rocket fuel.

I am not a waste of space, air, or time, and I never was, though admittedly, I have wasted a fair bit of time trying to figure out APA formatting.

And now. every time I walk into a classroom, a meeting, or a space where someone looks like they're trying to shrink into a desk, I remember that version of me. I carry him with me. And I try to be the voice that says, You can.

Harnessing ADHD as a Superpower

As I kept moving forward, clawing my way through each challenge, I began to discover something unexpected, a hidden alley in my constant war with dyslexia: my ADHD.

What had always been labeled a "disorder," a problem, something to be managed or medicated into submission, suddenly started to feel like a weapon I could sharpen and wield. I stopped viewing it as a burden and started leaning into it, especially the parts no one ever told me were useful. The energy. The intensity. The obsession. The ability to zero in on a task with such fierce focus that the world disappeared.

That hyper-focus, the kind that can make someone forget to eat, sleep, or notice the passage of time, became my secret weapon. When the reading was dense, when the writing was painful, when my eyes blurred from exhaustion and my brain screamed stop, ADHD stepped in and said, Let's go. It gave me an extra gear, a kind of mental overdrive that kicked in exactly when I needed it most. While others paced themselves, I sprinted, fueled by a mind that didn't know how to rest.

ADHD wasn't just some magical hidden gift. It also came with chaos. My thoughts could scatter like a flock of startled birds, darting in every direction, leaving me chasing one idea while ten others slipped away. I'd start a task only to derail into a side project that didn't matter, or I'd fixate on the wrong detail and miss the big picture. I made mistakes. I spun in circles. I wasted time trying to get out of my own head. But over time, I learned how to channel it.

I began building systems that helped me direct that energy. Timers, lists, color-coding, movement breaks, anything that gave my brain structure without caging it in. I figured out how to ride the wave of hyper-focus without drowning in it. I stopped fighting against my brain and started working with it, understanding its rhythm, its spikes and crashes, and how to harness its raw force into something productive.

When paired with the resilience I had developed from years of struggling with dyslexia, ADHD became my edge.

Turning Struggles into Strengths

None of this made the road easier, not by a long shot. It meant grinding harder than everyone else just to keep up, and even then, it often felt like I was still two steps behind. It meant late nights, long hours, and the kind of mental exhaustion that seeps into your bones. Success wasn't always some shiny celebration with perfect grades and accolades, sometimes it was a C on a paper I worked on for weeks. And I celebrated it like it was a damn A+.

Every assignment I completed was a fight. Every test I passed was a win. Every time I turned something in on time, even if it wasn't perfect, felt like defying gravity. I didn't need to be the best; I just needed to keep showing up, keep climbing, and keep proving to myself that I could. And I did.

I may not have had natural academic talent. I may not have written with ease or breezed through exams. But what I did have was grit. I had energy. I had drive. I had this fire in my gut that said, *don't quit*. And ADHD, once the thing that got me in trouble, became the fuel that kept that fire burning.

People love to throw around the word "disorder" like it's a dead-end. But ADHD, for me, was a roadmap. It taught me to think fast, move with urgency, adapt on the fly, and find solutions when none were obvious. It gave me the stamina to work late, the drive to keep pushing, and the creativity to approach problems in unconventional ways.

When paired with my coping tools, that energy stopped being something that held me back. It became a force that propelled me forward, faster, harder, and more determined than I ever thought possible.

What some saw as a weakness became one of my greatest strengths.

Because at the end of the day, it's not about how your brain should work, it's about how you learn to work with the brain you've got. And mine? It's wild. It's messy. But it gets the job done.

And that's more than enough.

Redefining Success

Looking back now, after all the battles, failures, and improbable wins, I've come to see something clearly, something I wish I had known much earlier in life: our differences don't have to be weaknesses. They're unrefined strengths, waiting to be understood, shaped, and used. They're the very things that, once embraced, can set us apart and carry us further than we ever imagined.

For me, ADHD became that strength. That edge. That tool I didn't know how to use until I'd stumbled enough times to figure it out. It gave me a kind of relentless fuel that helped me push past the limitations dyslexia tried to enforce. It drove me through academic hurdles, through nights filled with doubt, through failures that should have ended the story but didn't.

It wasn't talent that got me here. It wasn't luck. It was persistence. Grit. The daily choice not to quit. The decision to turn toward the fight instead of away from it.

I've proven a lot over the years, to professors, to teachers, to bosses, but mostly to myself. I proved that I could succeed where others thought

I would fail. That I could rewrite a future that was never supposed to belong to someone like me. That a kid with a messy report card, labeled and underestimated, could rise, not because he was naturally brilliant, but because he just wouldn't stop trying.

From undergrad failures to graduate school triumphs, from being laughed at by authority figures to finding my footing in professional circles, I picked up lessons that became the bedrock of who I am today. These weren't things I read in a book. They were hard-earned, carved out of experience, soaked in sweat, doubt, and persistence.

Resilience

Not the glossy, Instagram version. I'm talking about real resilience, the kind that drags you out of bed when you feel like you've already lost. The kind that whispers "try again" when everything in you is telling you to stop. Failure is only final if you decide it is. I learned that firsthand.

Adaptability

There is no one right way to learn, to think, to solve a problem. I had to stop comparing myself to the people who seemed to do everything with ease and started asking, what works for me? The answer wasn't always obvious, but the more I leaned into my differences, the more progress I made.

Weaponizing My ADHD

That's what I call it now. ADHD, once my greatest liability, became the engine that kept me moving. It gave me energy, a sense of urgency, and a bottomless well of effort I could tap into when the tank should have been empty. It didn't erase the challenges that came with dyslexia, but it gave me the power to fight through them.

The Power of Support

No one does this alone. I didn't. My wife stood by me when I couldn't even stand by myself. My mentors took the time to believe in me before I knew how to believe in myself. My colleagues saw the value I brought and encouraged me to keep going. Support doesn't erase the struggle, but it makes the burden lighter. It gives you just enough strength to take the next step.

Hard Work Over Talent

If I had waited to feel smart, I'd still be waiting. But I showed up. I stayed late. I asked questions. I tried again. And again. And again. In the end, it wasn't about being the most talented in the room. It was about being the one who refused to walk out of it.

That's how I redefined success, not by how easy it looked from the outside, but by how much I fought for it from the inside. My story isn't shiny or perfect. It's messy. It's full of failures, missteps, and reroutes. But it's also full of wins that came the hard way, earned, not given.

And that makes them mean so much more.

The University Years: A Turning Point

The university years weren't just a period of academic struggle; they were the turning point of my life. They cracked me open, exposed every weakness, tested every limit. But more importantly, they became the place where I finally rewrote the story I had been told my whole life. The one where I didn't belong. The one where I wasn't good enough.

I had every reason to quit. Dyslexia made even basic assignments feel like climbing Everest in flip-flops. ADHD tried to pull my focus in a thousand directions. And the ghosts of my past, teachers who dismissed me, instructors who ridiculed me, and a system that nearly buried me, they all echoed in my ears like a cruel chorus. You'll never make it. You're not college material. You should look into trade school.

But I didn't let those voices win. I pushed forward. I clawed my way up. Not because I was the smartest or the most talented, but because I was the most stubborn. I refused to be what they said I was. And slowly, something incredible happened.

The kid who had spent most of his life being underestimated, the one at the bottom of the class, the one who couldn't read out loud without stumbling, the one who sat in special ed classrooms feeling like a mistake, well, he earned a bachelor's degree. And then, kept going.

I earned my master's degree. I didn't just pass. I didn't just survive. I finished first in my cohort, the very first to cross that finish line. And when I did, I was overwhelmed with joy. I felt free.

And that's when it hit me, if I could do this, I could do almost anything.

I didn't have to be defined by my challenges. I could turn them into my fuel. I could rise because of them, not in spite of them.

Those years taught me how to fight for myself. How to believe in something better. How to hold on to a dream even when no one else could see it.

I may have been the underdog. But I finished the race, and I crossed that line with my head held high, heart full, and the unshakable belief that no challenge is too big when you refuse to quit. That, for me, was everything.

Your Challenges Don't Define You, Your Fight Does

To anyone who feels like the odds are stacked against them, I want you to know you are stronger than you realize. The journey will be hard. The path will be steep. But that doesn't mean success is out of reach. With the right mindset, the right strategies, and the right support system, you can turn your challenges into steppingstones toward success.

I'm living proof that with grit, determination, and the right people in your corner, you can achieve what others think is impossible. Your greatest triumphs are waiting, just on the other side of persistence. And when you reach them, you'll look back and see how every struggle, every setback, and every moment of doubt shaped you into the person you were meant to become.

For those like me reading this book, your challenges don't define you, your perseverance and courage do. Keep moving forward, even when it's hard. Because the moment you refuse to quit is the moment you begin to thrive.

Chapter 7

Dyslexia, Deadlines, and the Drive to Prove Them Wrong

Somehow, through grit, caffeine, late nights, and more than a few meltdowns, I made it. I clawed through junior year, limped through senior year, and eventually crossed the finish line with a diploma in hand. College nearly broke me, but it also taught me how to survive. That hard-earned resilience became the foundation I leaned on in graduate school, where the stakes were higher, the pressure more intense, and the imposter syndrome louder than ever.

If freshman year was rough, sophomore year was its evil twin, meaner, moodier, and far less forgiving. The hope I carried into college had already taken a beating, and I was just trying to hold myself together. It felt like running a marathon in flip-flops while everyone else glided by in Nikes. I had grit and a growing set of coping tools, but the weight of dyslexia, ADHD, and self-doubt never fully lifted. Even so, vending machines, strange roommates, caffeine-fueled nights, and small, unexpected victories kept me moving forward.

After earning my master's degree in 1997, I stepped into the world I had fought so hard to reach. Even before graduating, I had started working in my field, picking up short-term projects with firms like Dames & Moore, SAIC, and Knight & Leavitt. Those early gigs gave me a glimpse of what was possible. But after graduation, it was time to dive in, no training wheels, no safety net, just headfirst into the deep end.

After Knight & Leavitt, I took positions with Lockheed Martin and ICF Kaiser as a scientist, and they weren't just jobs. They were my proving grounds. The skills I had clawed together during years of academic struggle now had to stand tall in a competitive, high-pressure environment. Every lesson I had learned in graduate school, grit, adaptation, creative problem-solving, became the foundation of how I approached my work. But this transition was anything but smooth.

My old challenges didn't vanish once I stepped into a professional setting. Dyslexia and ADHD followed me like shadows, showing up in ways I hadn't expected. Writing technical reports became a battlefield. Grammar, spelling, sentence flow, all things others took for granted, were minefields I had to navigate daily. I struggled to catch the small mistakes that often-carried big consequences. My attention span buckled under the weight of long, technical tasks. My mind wanted to wander, to leap ahead, to shift tracks when I needed it to stay put.

What made it even harder was working alongside high-performing PhDs who didn't understand what I was fighting. Many of my supervisors were brilliant, but they had no framework for someone like me. They expected top-tier performance with minimal struggle, and when I fell short, their confusion sometimes felt like judgment. I wasn't asking for a free pass. I just needed understanding. What I got, more often than not, was pressure and scrutiny.

But I didn't let that stop me.

It took me twice as long to write a report, so I put in twice as many hours. I worked ten- to twelve-hour days to produce work that could stand beside that of my peers. I absorbed everything I could, from my supervisors, my colleagues, the projects, and the field. I became a sponge, refusing to let a single lesson slip past me. I focused not on what I couldn't do, but on how to turn what I *could* do into value.

Every challenge became a chance to grow. Every misstep became an opportunity to improve. I wasn't trying to be the best overnight; I was building something that would last. I wasn't the fastest. I wasn't the most naturally gifted. But I was relentless. And over time, that mattered.

Still, the doubts didn't vanish. They clung to me, whispering familiar lies from old teachers and instructors: You're not good enough. You'll never make it. And worse, I often looked for external validation, a supervisor's nod, a compliment, a sign that I was on the right track. But I learned quickly: in the real world, no one has time to hold your hand.

Expectations were clear: perform, deliver, adapt. That was it.

So, I stopped waiting for someone to tell me I was doing okay. I started telling myself. I traded approval for ownership. I stopped chasing validation and started chasing growth.

It was graduate school all over again, the pressure, the deadlines, the need to adapt constantly. But I had done it once, and I knew I could do it again. The resilience I had built through all those years of struggle became my armor in the workforce. I leaned into it.

Working at Lockheed and ICF Kaiser gave me structure, stability, and a window into how high-performing systems worked. But it also showed me something deeper about myself: I didn't just want to follow someone else's rules. I had my own vision, my own drive, and I wanted to create something of my own. Those years taught me how the world worked, and they also taught me that I was capable of building something better.

Little by little, things began to shift. My supervisors noticed my work ethic. They respected the way I kept showing up, pushing harder, learning faster. I may not have been the polished scientist they expected, but I was the one who refused to quit. And over time, that earned their respect.

I knew then that my future didn't lie in climbing someone else's ladder.

It was in building my own.

Navigating Environments with Dyslexia and ADHD

Entering the professional world with dyslexia and ADHD felt like being dropped into a foreign country where I didn't speak the language, but I was expected to be fluent, immediately. There was no time for translation, no margin for error. Everything moved fast, and the unspoken rule was clear: adapt or disappear.

I had spent years in school learning how to navigate around my challenges. I knew how to mask my dyslexia, how to anticipate the traps, how to blend in. But this was different. Here, in this world of deadlines and deliverables, no one was interested in your learning style or how hard you worked behind the scenes. Precision and speed weren't just goals, they were currency. There was no patience for flaws. Mistakes didn't come with feedback; they came with consequences.

I learned to hide, again. I edited every report five, six, seven times. I combed through each sentence like a minefield, praying I didn't miss something obvious. I spent my days double-checking, second-guessing, obsessing. And still, errors slipped through. A typo. A skipped word. A sentence that didn't quite track. Small things to most—but to me, they felt like cracks in the armor. Each one chipped away at my confidence and reinforced the fear I carried every day: You're not good enough. You don't belong here.

What I didn't realize at the time was that while dyslexia required me to slow down, my ADHD demanded the opposite. It pushed me to move faster, do more, take on everything at once. But instead of letting it sabotage me, I began to weaponize it. I leaned into the hyperfocus. I let the adrenaline pull me through long nights and 60+ hour weeks. I stayed late, came in early, and said yes to everything. My ADHD became the motor I strapped to my back to outrun the doubts. And for a while, it worked.

I delivered. I met deadlines. I solved problems with an intensity that others noticed, even if they didn't understand where it came from. I masked the struggle so well that people assumed I was just driven, tireless, maybe even brilliant. They didn't see the tightrope walk, the sheer exhaustion of pretending every single day.

Building Confidence as I Demonstrated My Value and Expertise

Confidence is a strange thing when you've grown up doubting your own mind. I didn't walk into the workplace believing I was smart. I walked in hoping I could fake it well enough to get by. Every project felt like a test I wasn't prepared for. Every meeting was a performance where I held my breath, waiting for someone to realize I didn't belong.

Fear, as it turns out, can be a powerful motivator. I pushed myself to overprepare, to overdeliver. I couldn't always be the fastest or the most articulate, but I could be the most committed. I became the person who stayed late, who checked and rechecked every detail, who quietly made sure the job got done. And slowly, people began to notice.

At first, it was small. A nod of appreciation. A compliment from a colleague. Then came bigger moments, being asked to lead projects, trusted with more responsibility. Each recognition was like a brick laid on a shaky foundation, slowly building a sense of worth I'd never fully known. I started to believe, maybe, just maybe, I had earned my place.

The turning point wasn't a grand success; it was a quiet realization. I wasn't being defined by my mistakes anymore. I was being seen for my work ethic, my consistency, my drive. For someone who had spent so much of their life hiding, that visibility was everything. It didn't just validate me, it hanged me.

Gaining Mentorship from Colleagues and Leaders Who Believed in My Potential

One of the smartest things I ever did was seek out the best minds in my field and attach myself to them. Not in a formal way, there were no mentorship programs or special introductions. I just showed up. I listened. I observed. And I studied their every move.

These were the people others admired from afar. I got close enough to learn how they thought, how they tackled problems, how they carried themselves in rooms where the stakes were high. I never told them I was dyslexic or that my brain often raced in twenty directions at once. I didn't need to. I just watched and absorbed.

I took on the grunt work without complaint. I asked questions when I could. I mirrored their approach and gradually began weaving their habits into my own routines. They didn't know it, but they were helping me rewrite the internal narrative I'd lived with for so long, that I was broken, that I had to hide, that success wasn't meant for people like me.

They never saw me as less-than. They saw my hunger to learn, my willingness to show up, and my refusal to quit. Their high standards didn't intimidate me; they gave me something to rise to. And through them, I found not just skills, but self-respect.

Eventually, I stopped copying them and started trusting my own instincts. I wasn't just learning anymore, I was becoming. Their guidance helped me shape a version of myself that could not only survive in this world but thrive.

Hiding in Plain Sight

Despite all the progress I made, one thing always nagged at me: I rarely saw anyone like me in my field. No one talked about dyslexia. No one admitted to having ADHD. I started to wonder, were they not here at all. Or were they, like me, hiding behind polished presentations and carefully edited reports?

Hiding is exhausting. Pretending not to struggle is its own full-time job. I did the same thing in public school. I hid so I would fit in, so I thought.

My dyslexia was never truly invisible. The signs were there, typos, disorganized notes, that occasional deer-in-the-headlights look during a fast-moving meeting. People noticed. They just didn't know what they were seeing. I learned to laugh it off, to redirect, to act unfazed. But inside, I was running damage control, always trying to stay one step ahead of being "found out."

I avoided reading aloud. Skimmed documents and nodded along, even when I was struggling to process the content. I had tricks, ways to pivot the conversation, to buy myself time, to avoid exposure. And while my ADHD gave me the energy to work around the clock, the emotional toll of constant concealment weighed on me in ways I didn't fully understand at the time.

No matter how hard I worked, I never fully shook the feeling that I was playing a role. That if people really knew what it took for me to keep up, they might not see me the same way. That fear sat in the background of every success, whispering that it was all temporary. That one day, the mask would slip.

Owning My Truth

I've learned that our differences don't make us less. They make us more. More determined. More resilient. More creative. We don't get to take the easy road, so we build our own.

I still triple-check my work. I still miss things. My brain still moves faster than my fingers can type. But I've stopped seeing that as a flaw. It's just part of the process. My process.

I've spent a career pretending things were easier than they were. But the truth is, my struggles shaped me. They forced me to work harder, to think differently, to adapt when others coasted. And over time, those things stopped being survival mechanisms, they became my strengths.

For anyone out there who feels like they're hiding in plain sight: I see you. I am you. And I promise, the things you think make you unqualified? They might just be the very things that make you exceptional.

Success didn't come from hiding. It came from the grit to keep going, the courage to show up, and the slow, hard-earned belief that I belonged. Not because I was perfect. But because I never stopped proving I was worth it; typos, tangents, and all.

Surviving the First Years: Grind, Grit, and a Lot of Rewrites

My early professional years weren't powered by brilliance. They were powered by brute-force persistence. With dyslexia and ADHD in the mix, nothing came easy. But I didn't need easy. I needed results. And I got them the only way I knew how: repetition, hard work, and a refusal to never stop moving forward.

While others polished their reports and went home at five, I was still there, editing, re-editing, double-checking spelling, and trying to make sure one rogue typo didn't derail the entire thing.

I didn't coast. I couldn't. I created my own formula for survival.

- **Repetition was my secret weapon.** I reread every report, sometimes aloud, sometimes backward, until the words stopped fighting me.
- **I worked longer and harder than most.** Ten- to twelve-hour days were the norm, not the exception.
- **I triple-checked everything.** Spelling, formatting, sentence flow, nothing got a free pass.
- **I learned from everyone.** I became a sponge, soaking up every process, technique, and best practice from colleagues and supervisors.
- **I adapted constantly.** If something didn't work for my brain, I tweaked it until it did. Color coding, pacing while reading, recording notes, whatever it took.

No one handed me success. I built it with slow, steady, often exhausting effort. I wasn't the fastest. I wasn't the flashiest. But I was relentless.

In the end, that's what made all the difference.

Taking a Leap: Starting My Own Firm

My time at ICF Kaiser was invaluable. I'd grown there, learned a ton, and earned real respect. But there was this pull, a whisper that kept getting louder: There's more. You can do more. Build something that's yours.

It wasn't a spontaneous leap. Oh no, I planned it. Meticulously. Obsessively. The wild twist? My wife was pregnant, and we had about enough money to fill a vending machine. So naturally, in classic ADHD fashion, I thought, now seems like a great time to start a company from scratch! Honestly, it was probably the craziest ADHD need I'd had up to that point, and that includes alphabetizing my garage tools at 3 a.m. instead of sleeping before a major meeting.

This wasn't about a little restlessness. This was a full-on, "ditch the manual, burn the map, build your own damn trail" moment. I needed space to roam, to create, to pace around a room with a tennis ball in one hand and a spreadsheet in the other. I needed a world where late-night ideas scribbled on napkins weren't just allowed, they were celebrated. And no matter how great my bosses were, none of them were signing off on "Doug's Chaos Lab" as a business model.

It wasn't that I couldn't succeed in the traditional workplace, I had. But it always felt like wearing someone else's shoes: stiff, uncomfortable, and definitely not my size. My brain zigzagged, leapt, made wild connections, and refused to move in straight lines. I finally realized… that wasn't a flaw. That was the engine.

I did the thing, started to build the firm that would define me....

April: I dreamed it up.

May: I built it.

June: The doors opened.

And in July of 1997, I officially incorporated my own environmental consulting firm.

Oh gosh, what have I done!

From that moment forward, I was all in. There was no Plan B, just grit, coffee, and the echo of "What have I done?" bouncing around my skull.

I didn't quit ICF Kaiser right away. Nope, I went full double life. Up at 5 a.m., at my desk by 6, out at 2 p.m., and then came the second shift.

I'd sprint across town, pick up soil samples, visit job sites, and finally end up at my tiny, rented office tucked into a corner of Las Vegas. It wasn't much, just a folding table, a coffee pot that coughed more than it brewed, and one stubborn guy with a dream.

I worked until 11 p.m. most nights, sometimes later. My hands in samples, my brain on fire with ideas. Somehow, even through the exhaustion, I felt alive. Because geochemistry was my world. It didn't care about my spelling. It didn't need flowery language. It just needed precision, focus, and obsession. And for once, my dyslexia wasn't a barrier, it was irrelevant.

ADHD became my hidden strength. I had energy for days. I could hyperfocus through the night while juggling client calls, paperwork, and seventeen Post-it notes. While others burned out, I just burned hotter. I didn't slow down; I didn't know how to slow down.

I made it a point to shake hands with every client, every single day. I visited offices, met them in the field, showed up whether they expected me or not. And when I ran into them at grocery stores or school events, you better believe I worked in a handshake and a follow-up. I cared about them. That relationship-first mindset became the heartbeat of the business.

And thanks to ADHD, I remembered things others forgot, what their dog's name was, that weird sediment sample from three months ago, the offhand comment they made about a project they'd shelved. I wasn't disorganized. I was connected. It was like my brain was building a spiderweb of information, and I was using every strand to keep the business strong.

At first, my only goal was simple: to make $5,000 a month. That felt massive. I maxed out credit cards. I borrowed $900 from my father-in-law just to get started. I didn't tiptoe into this. I cannonballed in with no safety net and nothing but adrenaline, stubbornness, and a shaky but determined plan.

My firm was only pulling in small pieces of projects, $30 per item, analyzing maybe six to eight samples a day, spread across three small clients. It wasn't glamorous, but it was steady. I treated each of those samples like they were gold bars. Every result was precise. Every report was on time, often within twenty-four hours. I was building a reputation, one data point at a time.

But at the three-month mark, everything changed. I landed with a big client, my second client of the company. Suddenly, I was processing seven to ten samples a day just from them. Overnight, I more than doubled my daily revenue. When that first full batch came in, I celebrated like a little kid on Christmas morning. I had been grinding, clawing, juggling bills and belief and now, finally, the word was out: I delivered. My edge over the established firm was made up of three parts. I had speed, quality, and I offered a lower cost.

No other firm in town could match all three. They may have offered one, maybe two. But never all three. That's what made me different, and it's what made me dangerous. That was my ADHD in action, hyperfocus, obsessive follow-through, and a brain that didn't know how to quit. I was in gear and flying.

Of course, success draws attention, and not all of it good.

My only real competitor at the time went full soap opera villain. He launched a crusade and tried to block me at every turn. At one point, he even sent letters to all my clients claiming I wasn't qualified to do geochemical analysis.

The guy didn't even have a college degree. Not one. When my clients opened that letter, they weren't just unimpressed. They were offended on my behalf. One even said, "This is like a guy with no driver's license telling me how to parallel park."

It backfired gloriously. Some forwarded me the letter with notes like,

> "Hey, thought you'd want a copy of your fan mail,"

or

> "Looks like you've got a full-time hype man!"

His sabotage attempts accidentally became my best marketing campaign. Free publicity, courtesy of envy and poor judgment. I was the new kid in town, and most people hadn't even heard of my company yet.

But now everyone knew there was a new option for their samples, one that delivered fast results, high quality, and at half the cost.

And then, it worked. Slowly, clumsily, but gloriously, it worked. The little office turned into a growing firm. I hired scientists and landed major contracts. And that blurry dream I once sketched on a notepad late at night eventually became a multimillion-dollar company.

For ten months, I lived a double life: full-time scientist by day, solo entrepreneur by night. I ran on fumes and pure belief. And then, thirty days after my first child was born, a time when most sane people would cling to the security of a steady paycheck, I quit my job.

That's right. Brand-new baby in one arm. Business license in the other. I leapt.

No safety net. No backup plan. Just full-blown, glorious chaos.

What a great wife to support me, or maybe she was just so sleep-deprived from being a new mom that she didn't have the energy to fully process what I was saying. Honestly, I think I caught her in that perfect postpartum fog where I could've said, "Hey, I'm quitting my job to become a professional yodeler," and she would've just nodded and said, "Okay, but can you bring home diapers?"

It was terrifying. It was exhilarating. It was completely unhinged. But I knew it was time.

I was building our future, one with room for my daughter to grow up seeing what possibility looks like when you say yes to it. Looking back, I'm still amazed by that version of me, half-delirious, always dusty, constantly forgetting what day it was. But I believed. I knew I was building something real. And if I had one secret weapon through it all, it wasn't a business degree or perfect grammar. It was my wife.

What kind of woman, nine months pregnant, stares down the financial chaos of a startup and says, "Sure, quit your job and follow your dream"?

Mine did.

Isn't that completely insane?

But she believed in me, before the first contract. Before the first dollar. Before I even fully believed in myself. She gave me strength.

I'd come homeate, exhausted and distracted, covered in dust and bad ideas. And still, she never complained. She held our newborn in one arm, my chaos in the other, and made it look effortless. She was the calm in my storm, and the reason I kept going when everything told me to stop.

Those early years were brutal. They were beautiful. And they built me.

Not just the business. Me. All because a woman said, *"Go for it."* It happened because a baby girl reminded me what the future could look like and because a relentless, hyperactive brain finally found a place to belong.

Facing the Challenges of Entrepreneurship

Entrepreneurship isn't easy. In fact, most days, it's painful, uncertain and full of moments that make you question your own sanity. But looking back now, I honestly think my ADHD gave me a kind of fearlessness, maybe even immunity, to the usual doubts that stop people from taking the leap. That impulsiveness, the part of me that never quite waited for permission or played it safe, pushed me forward when others might have pulled back. And my hyperactive nature gave me the stamina to chase dreams when a steady paycheck and a 9-to-5 would have sounded a whole lot more reasonable.

Stepping out on my own was equal parts thrilling and terrifying. I wasn't new to hard work, but starting a business was a different beast entirely. I had to become a fast learner in areas I'd never touched: client management, marketing, budgeting, risk. There wasn't a manual for how to do this with dyslexia and ADHD. No guide for how to keep the lights on while juggling invoices, project deadlines, and the weight of self-doubt. I learned by doing. Trial by fire. And yes, by making some downright foolish decisions that, to this day, my wife lovingly (and occasionally not-so-lovingly) reminds me of.

I always landed on my feet. I made mistakes, sure, but I never stopped trying. I never stopped dreaming. That stubbornness, some might call it delusion, was my lifeline.

The challenges were real. There were days when I sat alone in my tiny office, head in my hands, wondering if I'd made a huge mistake. Would the clients come? Could I keep up? Would my dyslexia betray me at the worst possible moment? Would ADHD leave me chasing too many threads and finishing none? These weren't passing thoughts, they were constant background noise. But the one thing louder than that fear was my determination.

Science kept me anchored. Specifically, geochemistry. It was my sweet spot. Unlike school, there were no red pens marking up my writing or grammar rules to memorize. The work spoke for itself. Data didn't care how I spelled. Results didn't need to be poetic. I could hyper-focus for hours, lost in numbers, analyses, real-world problems I could actually solve. For the first time, my brain felt like it wasn't working against me, it was working with me.

Still, hiding my challenges wasn't easy. In fact, it was exhausting. I worried, constantly, about how I was being perceived. What if clients saw a mistake in a report? What if staff noticed I was circling back on things three, four, five times? What if someone saw the cracks I was working so hard to patch?

Even now, those insecurities linger. I carry the scars of a thousand tiny humiliations from school and early career ridicule. The jokes about typos. The raised eyebrows. The subtle doubt. That kind of thing doesn't leave quietly. It turns into hypervigilance, into perfectionism. I poured all of that anxiety into making sure nothing was out of place. If my work was airtight, maybe no one would see the chaos behind it.

Even with all that worry, I knew one thing with absolute certainty: I was a damn good scientist. Dyslexia didn't stop me from thinking critically or solving complex problems. It just made me take the long way around. I had to work harder, double-check everything, and find ways to translate my ideas into a format the world could understand. But my ideas were solid. My instincts were sharp, and my passion was unmatched.

Running the business meant wearing every single hat, sometimes all in the same day. I was the field tech, the analyst, the report writer, the janitor, the invoice generator, the client whisperer. I was also the guy loading soil samples in the heat and negotiating contracts in the same sweaty shirt. It was chaos, but it was my chaos. And my ADHD, once the thing teachers and bosses struggled to "manage," became my superpower. I had the energy to work long hours, the mental flexibility to switch tasks on a dime, and the excitement to chase every opportunity with reckless enthusiasm.

Client outreach wasn't some chore I saved for Fridays. It was woven into every moment. I'd be grabbing lunch with my kids at McDonald's and spot a potential client. I'd strike up conversations at grocery stores, at stoplights, even in the middle of pushing a cart through a hardware aisle. I couldn't help it. My brain was always on, always scanning for connections. It made for some wild stories and a few eye rolls from my wife, but it also kept the business growing.

I'll never forget a conversation with my first client, Mel Babcock, a sharp, seasoned geotechnical engineer who, for reasons still unclear, decided I was worth taking a chance on. Now, Mel wasn't your average buttoned-up, clipboard-carrying engineer. The man had a beer keg in his office. Not a fridge. Not a six-pack. An actual, functioning keg.

Every few days around 5 p.m., I'd swing by his office, partly for work talk, but mostly for the free pints. It became a ritual: me, Mel, and his crew sipping cold beer, talking shop, and occasionally swapping wildly inappropriate job site stories. It was during one of these golden-hour happy hours, foam-topped pint in hand, that Mel looked over and said:

"Doug, you'll always have issues with employees and colleagues because your work ethic, drive, and thinking is way outside the box."

I didn't know whether to be flattered or mildly roasted. Was that a compliment or an intervention?

Beer buzz aside, Mel was right. My brain didn't operate like most people's. It was like a pinball machine with a caffeine addiction. I worked differently. I moved fast. I expected intensity and borderline obsession, because that's what I brought to the table. And when others didn't, I struggled to understand why they weren't sprinting alongside me like their lives depended on it.

It took time, a lot of time for me to realize that not everyone needed to operate like me to be valuable. That different rhythms weren't a threat, they were the reason teams work. Turns out, variety is good. Who knew? Learning to value those differences made me a better leader, a better colleague, and a better person who sometimes lets people leave work before sunset.

Looking back, what started as a half-mad leap into the unknown became the most fulfilling chapter of my life other than marriage and kids. I went from barely surviving to thriving. I built something from scratch, something real, something that reflected my values, my brain, and my slightly chaotic but very determined belief that I could pull it off.

And Mel was right. Again. Also, with lots of pints of good beer.

Dyslexia and ADHD didn't stop me. They shaped me. They gave me angles no one else saw, energy no one else matched, and a kind of resilience you can only earn the hard way. What most people once called a deficit became the engine of everything I've built.

And it bears repeating--none of it, absolutely none of it, would've been possible without my wife. She believed in me when the odds looked terrible. She endured the late nights, the wild ideas, the forgotten details, and the endless stream of half-finished projects with grace and a kind of quiet strength I still don't understand. She both tolerated and supported my chaos. She saw the dream when all I could see were the risks. And for that, I am endlessly, profoundly grateful.

Together, we turned a blurry vision into a life we are proud of. A life that was never conventional, never simple, but always ours.

Building a Company: Growth, Success, and the Road to Sale

What began as a one-man operation in a rough part of town, fueled by caffeine and blind ambition, somehow evolved into a legitimate business. That first office, if you could call it that, was sandwiched between trouble and survival. There were drug dealers on the corners, the homeless drifting through, and working girls negotiating their nights out in the open. It was unpolished and definitely not the kind of place you'd expect to birth a multimillion-dollar company. But that's exactly what happened.

It wasn't glamorous. Sometimes it wasn't even safe. But it was mine. That little space, with its buzzing fluorescent lights and cracked linoleum floors, became my starting line. Every long night spent analyzing samples, every early morning prepping for site visits, every detail, that office absorbed it all. It held the scrappy beginnings of a business that would one day become something far greater than I ever expected.

By mid-1998, things were picking up. Larger projects. More clients. Bigger contracts. I was still running full throttle, trying to do it all myself, but it was becoming clear that I couldn't keep up alone. That's when Mel Babcock's voice came back to me. His words haunted me and challenged me:

At the time, I hadn't fully grasped what he meant. I thought it was a compliment, maybe even a badge of honor. But now, as I stood on the edge of scaling my business, I realized it was a warning too. Bringing other people into my dream wasn't just about extra hands. It meant surrendering control, learning to trust, and accepting that not everyone would run as hot as I did.

Still, in classic ADHD fashion, I made a huge decision without a second thought. I brought in someone I barely knew and handed him 30 percent ownership of the company. On paper, it made sense. It helped with cash flow during the lean months, and it meant he had skin in the game. But in practice, let's just say I learned a lot.

While I was burning the midnight oil, powered by Diet Coke and sheer adrenaline, he was a clock-out-at-five guy. I'd be working through dinner, troubleshooting field data or prepping for the next day's inspections, and he'd be gone, already halfway through a beer. It drove me insane. I didn't want to micromanage, but I also didn't want to feel like I was dragging the company uphill by myself.

The urge to throw a stapler across the office was real. But staplers cost money, and I didn't have extra cash for tantrums. So, I adapted.

I forced myself to learn how to work with someone who didn't operate the way I did. I had to let go of this fantasy that everyone would match my energy, my intensity, and my obsession with perfection. I started to understand what Mel meant, deep in my bones. My partner wasn't lazy or incompetent; he just functioned differently. He was task-focused, consistent, and reliable with deliverables. He just wasn't built for leadership or managing staff. And his communication with staff was rough, to say the least. I became the buffer, smoothing over conflicts, running interference between him and the team, trying to maintain cohesion without losing my mind.

It wasn't easy, but it was necessary. He didn't share my vision for the business, but he helped keep it afloat during its most fragile stage. And over time, I learned to appreciate what he could do, rather than resent what he couldn't.

As the company grew, so did my role. I transitioned from being the one who did everything to the one who built the team. I hired scientists, field techs, and administrative support. I moved from the field to the strategy table. Slowly, we stopped just surviving and started thriving. Revenue climbed. Our name began to carry weight in the environmental consulting world. Clients trusted us, and our work started speaking for itself.

Of course, the road wasn't smooth. There were months when we barely made payroll, when projects went sideways, and when staff members didn't work out. But my ADHD-fueled drive wouldn't let me quit. I outworked every problem. I wore every hat, and I kept the dream alive with a kind of energy that felt endless, because it had to be.

That energy, the thing I was once told would be my downfall, became my superpower. My ADHD gave me the ability to juggle chaos, pivot fast, and push through exhaustion. It made me relentless. And in this business, relentless wins.

By 2004, we had built something real, a profitable firm, a respected brand, and a team that could stand on its own. And for the first time in years, I paused long enough to look around and realized I'd done it. It was time to let go.

Selling the business wasn't just about money. It was about the journey. My partner and I went our separate ways, partly because of our differences, but not without appreciation. He'd played a role, an important one, and for that, I'm grateful.

Looking back now, what I built was more than a company. It was proof that someone with dyslexia, ADHD, and a history of being underestimated could do more than just survive the professional world. I had carved a path that didn't exist for someone like me and walked it with everything I had.

The experience taught me how to lead, how to trust, and how to work with people who didn't think like I did. And more importantly, it taught me that my so-called "disabilities" weren't barriers. They shaped how I built, how I solved problems and how I led.

From a sketchy office in a forgotten part of town to a thriving firm known across the region, this wasn't just a business story. It was my becoming. And I'd do it all again in a heartbeat.

Struggles Shaped My Work Ethic and Leadership Style

Still, ADHD remained both my engine and my shadow. It gave me energy and creativity, allowed me to see patterns and opportunities where others saw chaos. But it could also overwhelm the people around me. I'd come in hot with new ideas, half-baked plans, and the kind of urgency that made others' heads spin. I had to learn, really learn, that not everyone thrived under pressure. That my speed wasn't everyone's speed. That leadership wasn't just about drive; it was about restraint.

But even the best systems can't always protect you from your own wiring.

About three years into running my firm, my ADHD threw open the door, hijacked the meeting, and lit a metaphorical fire in the breakroom. I was in full-on visionary mode, launching new services in our certified analytical laboratory, redesigning internal systems, and pivoting toward a high-risk, high-reward model for growth. And I did it all without telling my business partner.

The funny part was my wife knew, and she was watching the chaos unfold like it was a Netflix drama, except the plot twist was that I was spending our personal money to fund the buildout, because the business had none. My partner had no idea what was happening, and neither did the staff, who were trying to keep up with my mile-a-minute ideas and rapid-fire decisions.

I was blissfully unaware that I'd put everyone in a supercharged race with no guardrails. I assumed people could keep up. I didn't build consensus; I built confusion. My intentions were solid, growth, innovation, momentum, but the execution was a hot mess.

That season taught me one of the hardest truths in leadership: success can collapse under the weight of miscommunication and unbridled speed. ADHD had given me the vision, but without checks, it cost me nearly everything I built.

The ironic part was that when I later read about other entrepreneurs who built massive, successful companies, I noticed the same pattern. It turns out, this kind of unchecked momentum isn't rare, it's practically a rite of passage. But that doesn't mean it's sustainable.

After that, I changed my approach. I slowed down, just enough to be intentional. I brought others in earlier, explained the vision more clearly, listened more carefully. I still moved fast, but now I had people around me to help me steer. And most importantly, I started asking not just "Can we do this?" but "Should we do this, and who needs to be in the loop before we hit launc*h*?"

Entrepreneurship: Thriving Despite the Doubters

Starting my own firm was a full-blown declaration: I can do this. Even if you don't believe in me.

And let me tell you, a lot of people didn't.

The doubts weren't subtle. They weren't whispered behind closed doors. They came straight to my face.

"Why would you try that? It's too risky."

"You'll never make it."

"You should stick with a steady paycheck."

"You're going to fail."

They weren't asking if I might stumble. They were waiting for it.

Then came the calls. The smug, thinly veiled curiosity.

"How's that little business of yours going?"

"You still trying to make that work?"

At first, it pissed me off. Then it pushed me.

I'd respond with sarcasm, my armor of choice.

"Oh yeah, total failure over here. Just waiting for the big implosion."

I'd hang up the phone, unleash a symphony of four-letter words that would make a sailor blush, and a priest reconsider his life choices, get it all out of my system, and then dive right back into work like nothing happened. It was my own version of emotional detox; equal parts profanity and productivity.

But behind the jokes, I was burning with purpose. I worked harder than I ever had. I poured my energy into that business like it was my life raft, because in many ways, it was. My ADHD became the battery pack. My stubbornness became a strategy. And my past became fuel.

Where others saw risk, I saw opportunity. While they tiptoed, I jumped headfirst. I didn't always know the next move, but I trusted I'd figure it out on the way down. That's the gift ADHD gave me: motion. And motion beats perfection every time.

Eventually, the calls slowed. The questions faded. The people who once waited for me to fail stopped asking altogether. For a while, I was confused, why the silence?

Then it hit me: their doubt was never about me. It was about them. My willingness to leap reminded them of the chances they didn't take. And once it became clear I wasn't crashing, they didn't know what to say anymore.

From Misfit to Leader

Looking back now, I see that my struggles weren't obstacles to overcome. They were part of the path. Dyslexia made me careful, thoughtful, and inventive. ADHD made me relentless, visionary, driven.

Together, they forced me to build a team, not around my ego, but around my needs, a team that would not hide my flaws, but complement them. And that team helped me turn a small idea into a real company, with real impact.

I wasn't supposed to make it. At least that's what the doubters said. But I did, not because I did it despite my challenges, but because I did it with them. And the best part was I brought others with me, people who had also been overlooked, underestimated, or written off. And together, we built something that mattered.

The Root of Their Doubts

When I left the safety of a steady paycheck to bet on myself, I noticed something strange. People around me, family, friends, even former colleagues, started acting differently. They weren't angry or overtly critical. They were uncomfortable.

I think my decision stirred something in them, something they didn't want to look at too closely. Because when you step outside the expected path, when you risk everything to chase a dream, it forces others to examine why they never did.

For many, what I was doing was unimaginable. They couldn't picture themselves ever doing it, let alone succeeding. And deep down, I believe some of them wanted me to fail, not out of malice, but because my success would shine a light on their inaction. It would challenge the comfort they'd settled into and call out the dreams they'd abandoned long before.

Their doubts weren't really about me. They were about them. Their own fears and their own regrets.

They stayed in the safe zone, collecting paychecks, clocking in and out of jobs that offered stability but little else. There's nothing wrong with that. Not everyone is meant to take the leap. But I wasn't built to sit in someone else's office, waiting for someone else to decide what I was worth. I had to try. I had to know what I was capable of.

ADHD: My Secret Ingredient

People talk about ADHD like it's a liability, and for me, it was at first. Yet, in many ways, it's become my unfair advantage and secret ingredient.

Sure, it's messy. I've started more half-baked projects than I care to admit. I've chased ideas down rabbit holes, rearranged my desk at 2 a.m. because I had to, forgotten meetings, and interrupted more conversations than I'd like to admit.

ADHD also gave me something rare, and that is motion. I didn't wait. I moved. I chased opportunities most people wouldn't dare to touch. I took leaps before the landing pad was even built. And while others stood at the edge, weighing the risk, I was already midair, figuring it out.

That impulsiveness and restlessness built my business. It kept me up late, fueled by creativity and Diet Coke, dreaming up solutions and reaching out to clients when most people had already shut down for the day.

Redefining What Leadership Looks Like

Starting with my own environmental consulting firm was a personal revolution. It shifted how I saw myself and how I saw others who, like me, didn't fit the typical mold.

I began to see a pattern. Many of the most successful people I met, the ones breaking new ground, solving tough problems, redefining industries, were wired like I was. They/we were neurodivergent, unconventional, and misunderstood.

These weren't people who had followed someone else's blueprint. They were the ones writing new ones. They didn't thrive in rigid systems. They thrived in chaos, in ambiguity, and in the gray areas where creativity ruled.

I realized that in business, thinking differently is the engine of innovation. The world doesn't reward conformity. It rewards courage. It rewards flexibility, vision, and the ability to adapt when everything around you is falling apart.

From Limitations to Superpowers

There was a time when I saw my dyslexia and ADHD as burdens. In school, they were the reasons I stayed up late, the reasons I was misunderstood, and the reasons I was humiliated.

But in business they became my edge.

Dyslexia made me a creative problem solver. It helped me see around corners others didn't even know were there. I didn't think linearly, I thought laterally. I spotted patterns, and I connected dots others missed.

ADHD gave me the drive to keep moving, the capacity to handle chaos, the stamina to outlast, and the curiosity to outthink.

What once felt like limitations revealed themselves to be the very traits that made me unstoppable.

Thriving Through Adaptation

What really separates success from failure is adaptability.

I never clung to a failing plan. If something didn't work, I changed it. If a door closed, I built a window. When faced with a problem, I pivoted.

That mindset became the heartbeat of my company. I encouraged it in my team. I hired people who didn't need step-by-step instructions, but who thrived when given freedom. I didn't want robots, I wanted thinkers, people who challenged assumptions and who weren't afraid to break the rules in the name of a better outcome.

Over time, I realized something profound. I wasn't alone. The business world is full of people like me. People who've spent their whole lives being told they were "too much," "too scattered," "too intense." And yet, there we were, running companies, launching ideas, and changing industries. And one of shared qualities was that we didn't fit the mold.

Power of Neurodivergence in Business

Being neurodivergent is the thread that's been woven into every success I've ever had. It's the secret sauce; the untamed fire that's helped me see possibilities where others saw roadblocks. It allowed me to find creative solutions to problems no one else could crack and push forward when the path ahead looked more like a cliff than a road.

Far from being a limitation, my ADHD and dyslexia became the tools that set me apart. They were certainly tools I didn't ask for, but ones I learned to sharpen with time, resilience, and a hell of a lot of mistakes. These traits I'd been taught were quirks were actually my edge. They helped me build a business I believed in and make a real contribution to an industry I care deeply about.

Looking back, I realize something that would've blown my younger self's mind: the very traits that made school feel like a battlefield, sitting still, reading out loud, staying organized, meeting expectations I could never quite reach, were are the same traits that gave me the fuel to build, grow, and thrive in the business world.

What made me an outlier in traditional environments became my greatest advantage in an unstructured one.

The most important lesson I've learned is that success never came from trying to think like everyone else. It came from embracing the way I naturally think, which is differently.

The world's greatest innovators didn't earn their place by coloring inside the lines. They made their own colors. They redefined the rules. They leaned into the things that made them different, not despite the pushback, but because of it.

Owning My Wiring

For too many painful years, I believed my brain was broken. ADHD made it hard to focus. Dyslexia made it hard to write. Together, they made even the simplest tasks feel like climbing uphill in a windstorm, backward, blindfolded, and carrying a backpack full of doubt.

I used to think I had to work around who I was just to survive the day. That success meant hiding the struggle, compensating, and pretending. I believed I had to become someone else just to fit in.

But somewhere along the way, something shifted.

I stopped trying to "fix" myself and started listening to myself.

I stopped hiding and started owning who I am, quirks, challenges, and all that goes with it: me.

I realized that my differences weren't weaknesses.

They were the reason I saw the world differently. They were my edge.

No, I'm not a billionaire. I didn't build a tech empire. I didn't revolutionize an industry. But I built something that mattered. I created a business from nothing. I hired incredible people. I served clients with integrity. I showed up, every single day, and gave it everything I had.

I carved out a space where I belonged, not by changing who I was, but by finally embracing it.

Despite every person who said I'd never make it, every teacher who said I wasn't trying hard enough, every moment I doubted my own worth, I did it. I succeeded not by becoming someone else, but by becoming more fully myself.

So no, I'm not a household name. But I've built something real. And for a kid who once felt like he'd never measure up, that's a success you can't put a price on.

Building Differently, Leading Differently

As I built my business, I started attracting people who, like me, didn't exactly color inside the lines. People who squinted at the rulebook, shrugged, and said, "Eh, we can build a better one." They didn't fit the mold, and thank God, because molds are for Jell-O and mediocre thinking.

These were kindred spirits. Some had resumes, some had tattoos of obscure Star Wars quotes, but all of them had something. And once I stopped trying to build a "normal" team and started building a real one, everything changed.

I learned that when you make space for people to be exactly who they are; quirks, caffeine dependencies, rogue sticky notes, and all, you build magic and loyalty. You build a squad that will go to battle with you and maybe build a spreadsheet while riding a unicycle if that's what it takes.

Redefining Success: Spoiler: It's Not About Blending In

There was a time I measured success by how well I could pass for "normal." I measured it by how invisible I could make the struggle and how smoothly I could fake my way through small talk at networking events without screaming internally.

Now, I define success by impact, by the people I've helped, by the risks I've taken, and by the moments I chose action over perfection, and stubborn courage over comfort.

Changing the World (With Our Wild, Glorious Brains)

More and more, the world is waking up to what many of us have always known: the so-called "disorders" people like me carry are actually my misunderstood edge.

Creativity. Tenacity. Laser-focus (at 2 a.m.). A refusal to accept the world as it is. These aren't glitches in the system They're features.

Look at Branson and Jobs or many others. They didn't get where they are by following the crowd. They led it. They annoyed the system, disrupted the status quo, and built futures no one else could see.

If you've ever been told you think too differently, talk too fast, move too much, dream too big, hear me loudly and clearly. You're not broken. Perhaps you're built for something bigger.

Yes, the path will be harder. You'll trip. You'll doubt. You'll probably lose your keys and your train of thought at least twice a day. But it'll be your path and your version of greatness. I believe that's what changes the world, one gloriously wired brain at a time.

Believing in Yourself—Especially When No One Else Does

If life has taught me anything, it's that you have to believe in yourself even when no one else does, especially then.

You need to stop letting other people's voices shape your path and to stop trying to live under their ceiling of expectations. When someone says, "You can't," work harder in your own way. It's not ideal, and I'm the first to tell you that having to prove those in authority wrong doesn't make you feel warm and fuzzy about them or you. Many times, I would tell my doubters off with every four-letter word I could, well, in my head at least.

Believing in yourself won't instantly get rid of your doubt, but it will help you keep going. I still have those quiet moments, those internal echoes of every person who once underestimated me, and you probably will to. The more you learn to fight back, the easier it will be to drown out their voices with the sound of your own effort.

Protecting Your Fire

Another lesson I learned, sometimes the hard way, is that who you surround yourself with matters a lot.

Negativity is contagious, and so is doubt. If you let people into your circle who drain your energy, amplify your insecurities, or celebrate your failures, you won't last. They'll pull you down with a well-placed word or two or twenty. I've seen it, I've felt it, and I've walked away from it.

You have to protect your fire. You need people around you who lift you and challenge you, people who remind you who you are and what you're capable of on the days you forget. That kind of support, the kind I've been lucky enough to get from my wife, is priceless.

Surround yourself with doers, people who don't need you to feel so that they can feel good about their own unsatisfying lives. Positivity spreads and nourishes. When people confirm your positive feelings about yourself, you all win.

Refusing to Quit

The key to everything I've built and every shred of belief I've wrestled into place, boils down to one thing. I never quit. That's it. I didn't have a more sophisticated plan, so I stuck to this one, even when it got really hard, and my to-do list looked like a CVS receipt.

Trust me, you will want to quit. The opinions of others will linger and mix with your self-doubt. They'll whisper that you're not cut out for this. They will tell you outright or imply that you're too loud, too weird, too you to do more than what's expected of you. But remember why they're doing that. We've already talked about it. Most of that noise has nothing to do with you. It's just their own fear of failure, shrink-wrapped and projected onto your dreams.

Even when quitting seemed like the easier option, I kept going, and so can you. Success is not reserved for the valedictorians or the pedigreed. It's not about whether your emails use the Oxford comma correctly, or if you even know what the Oxford comma is. It's about refusing to sit down when everything tells you to fold.

As you may have already figured out, I'm not a clean-cut, overnight-success story. I'm the scrappy, coffee-stained, typo-prone version with dirt under my nails and a calendar that looks like a conspiracy theory. If I can do it, there's all kinds of hope for you. I'm proof that with enough stubbornness, enough fire, and a big enough chip on your shoulder, you can turn every "you can't" into a "watch me."

And if someone like me can make it, after the red pens, the detentions, the missed assignments, the low expectations, the flunkouts, and the chaos, so can you.

Now, get out there and make some noise.

Mentoring Others Who Face Similar Struggles

I didn't do this alone.

That needs to be said first, because the truth is, without the people who believed in me, especially when I struggled to believe in myself, I don't know where I'd be. At every stage of this journey, there were hands on my shoulders, sometimes steadying me, sometimes pushing me forward. They include my wife, my mentors, my colleagues, all of them who saw something in me I hadn't yet seen in myself.

The most valuable thing they offered me was belief. When you've spent most of your life being underestimated, misjudged, or told you wouldn't make it, that belief stays with you. It becomes the light you reach for when around you feels dark.

It's because of these people and their belief in me that I made it a personal mission to pay it forward. I know what it feels like to sit in a classroom and feel behind before the lesson even starts. I know what it's like to carry the invisible weight of learning challenges and to feel like your brain is wired wrong in a world that demands you think and act like everyone else. I know what it's like to be underestimated so often that you start to believe maybe everyone else is right. But I also that success is possible. Now, I devote a big part of my life to mentoring those who are walking that same hard road; those with dyslexia, ADHD, or simply a sense that the odds are stacked against them. I want to help them believe they can succeed. My heart is with them because I was them.

A Mission to Mentor

This is why I mentor every student I can, struggling or not. Everyone carries something. Everyone has a fight inside them, and with the right kind of support and a spark of self-belief, that fight can become something incredible.

I can still picture the faces of the people who believed in me when I didn't believe in myself. I remember them because they saw past the noise. They looked beyond the grades, the typos, the scattered energy, and they saw me. Not the version the world had labeled. The real me, buried under years of doubt and damage.

One of those people was Dr. Geof Spaulding. We didn't always see eye to eye. In fact, most of the time, we didn't. And back when I first worked with him early in my career, I don't think he fully saw what I was capable of. Still, he challenged me. He showed me what it meant to be a scientist. He lit the first spark.

Years later, after I'd made the jump into higher education, our paths crossed again. This time, we worked together on the first discovery of Ivanpah Lake, a late Pleistocene feature along the Nevada-California border. And something shifted. This time, he saw me.

He told me I'd seen what others hadn't, what no one else had noticed about Ivanpah. Coming from him, that recognition meant the world. It was validation from someone I'd once tried so hard to prove myself to.

Turning Struggles into Secret Weapons

To the people I mentor now, I say this. Your challenges don't define you, but how you face them does.

Your learning difference, your self-doubt, your anxiety are not flaws, but, like it or not, they are your battlefields. Every time you show up, every time you try again, every time you work through the hard stuff instead of running from it, you're winning a war most people never even see.

I share my story not to impress anyone, but to show the people I mentor and you, my reader, that the road is real, and so is the success at the end of it. I want you to know that with creativity, tenacity, and an unshakable work ethic, you can do things you once thought impossible.

I'm not making light of this because I've lived it, yet I truly believe that your difference might be the very thing that sets your apart, in the best way. Finally, and most important, the only voice that gets to define you is your own.

The Truth About Success

People often think success is for the lucky ones, the naturally talented, and the well-connected. The truth is, success is earned. It's built in silence and struggle. It's won by the ones who show up when it's hard, who keep going when no one's watching, and who learn to bet on themselves when no one else will.

My dyslexia, my ADHD, and the years I spent being overlooked, underestimated, and doubted, shaped me. They taught me how to fight, how to adapt, and how to rise when everything around me told me to stay down.

The Legacy I Want to Leave

Today, I carry every lesson forward. I mentor. I speak, and I support because I believe the most important thing I can do with my success is use it to light the path for someone else.

I want my story to be a signal flare for every kid who thinks they'll never measure up and for every adult who still hears the echo of childhood doubt. I want it to be there for every neurodivergent dreamer who's afraid to take the leap.

Success belongs to the ones who are willing to fight for it, to work harder, and to believe when no one else does.

If that's you, if you're different, underestimated, or written off, I want you to bet on yourself. Work harder than anyone else. Keep going, even when it's hard.

Chapter 8

How Love Became My Anchor

S uccess wasn't forged in solitude. Despite what every motivational poster or movie montage might try to sell you; motivation and hard work alone won't get you to the finish line. If that were true, I'd be writing this from the top of Mount Everest with a laptop powered by sheer stubbornness. As I've said many times to as many people who will hear me, what got me here wasn't just hustle or caffeine-fueled all-nighters. It was people, the ones who saw the chaos and didn't flinch. They stayed.

I didn't build a business alone, and I never would've made it without the people who walked beside me. Behind every bold risk, every near-burnout moment, there was someone quietly holding the net. Someone handing me coffee, calm, and unconditional belief. Especially my wife, God bless her. She has been the emotional air traffic control tower of my life. She's been my editor, my therapist, my tech support, my accountability partner, and my go-to sandwich distributor when I forget to eat for ten hours straight. She was the scaffolding I rebuilt myself around. When I couldn't see a future, she held the blueprint.

There's one night I'll never forget when I was back in college after my second academic suspension, trying to claw my way toward a passing grade. I sat at the kitchen table staring at a blank Word document, a paper due in less than twelve hours, and absolutely nothing to show for it. Not a title. Not an outline. Not even an ironic meme to ease the tension. My brain felt like overcooked scrambled eggs.

She just sat down next to me, no judgment in her voice, and said, "You talk. I'll help you write."

That was the night everything changed.

She helped me structure sentences, and she helped me breathe. She e taught me how to believe in myself again. Through every panic spiral and insecure grunt, every meltdown that began with "This is garbage!" and ended with "Why am I like this," she stayed. Later, during the final stretch of my PhD, the unthinkable happened. My dissertation lived on a hard drive that decided to die spectacularly. No backup, of course, and No cloud. Four years of work vanished in a single blue screen. I spiraled, full ADHD panic mode, complete with pacing, swearing, and a sincere declaration that I was going to become a park ranger and yell at raccoons.

She didn't panic. She focused, and then she focused me. We found a recovery service, overnighted the drive, and prayed. A week later, a miracle arrived: my dissertation, resurrected from the ashes of corrupted silicon. Without her, I wouldn't have made it to that defense. I wouldn't have made it, period.

Dyslexia and ADHD are challenges for everyone who shares life with me. It's not just forgotten keys or a hyperactive monologue at 2 a.m. It's motion without pause, ideas without anchors, and emotions that hit like pop-up thunderstorms.

Still, relationships weren't always smooth. When your mind runs on multiple tracks at once, communication can get interesting. And that's where the quirks of neurodivergence became both a challenge and a surprising gateway to connection.

My wife was and is the calm to my chaos, the lighthouse when I am lost at sea. She's not the only one.

Over the years, I've been blessed by a ragtag crew of fellow misfits, loyal friends, and the kind of professors who saw through the mess to the mind underneath. People like Dr. Kreamer, Dr. Hodge (rest in peace), and even the initially skeptical Dr. Spaulding. They didn't care that I couldn't spell "photosynthesis" on the first try. They cared that I understood it and could teach it with fire in my belly.

Friendships mattered just as much, maybe more. Not everyone stayed, and I've made peace with that. But the ones who saw the tangled thoughts, the typo-riddled notes and late texts, the squirrel-brain spirals, and still showed up are the ones who taught me what loyalty really means.

Dyslexia and ADHD follow me into relationships, and they also led the charge, proudly waving the flag of distraction. I once tried to fix a friendship with a meme. Seriously. My friend was hurt by something I said, and instead of addressing it directly, I sent a funny image about emotional damage and duct tape. In my mind, it was heartfelt. To them, it felt like a deflection.

I've interrupted deep conversations with sudden dives into sediment transport or the environmental impact of PFAS in drinking water, because, apparently, nothing says "I care about you" like microplastics and groundwater contamination. These weren't just random facts; they were my way of reaching out using the only language I sometimes had available: science, curiosity, and chaos.

Living with ADHD and dyslexia shaped how I learned as well as how I related to people. Sometimes awkward and often messy, those moments became windows into connection I never saw coming.

But buried in those mental zigzags, those ADHD-fueled shifts and dyslexic reroutes, were moments of magic. Raw, unfiltered connection. Unexpected laughter. A shift in perspective. Sometimes, it's in the unplanned moments, the ones that don't make it into the syllabus of life, where real learning and connection happen.

So how does this all tie into strength? That's because I've come to realize that true strength is knowing when to pause and let someone else meet you where you are. It's not about building walls to hide everything that's not working. It's about letting someone climb over, sit beside you in the mess, and say, "I get it."

I feel that "Success isn't built alone, it's built by the people who stay when your world feels like it's falling apart."

So, here's what I've learned:

- Success doesn't always wear a cape. Sometimes it wears sweatpants and brings you coffee.
- Love isn't about being perfect. It's about being present.
- Loyalty isn't loud. It's consistent.
- Real connection doesn't happen in bullet points (not even these). It happens in the margins.

And when you find your people, the ones who stay, who believe, who build with you when everything feels like it's crumbling, hold them tightly. Feed them snacks. Apologize when you go full chaos mode and thank them for riding the rollercoaster with you.

If you're trying to climb your own impossible mountain, don't do it solo.

Find your crew. Let them in. Let them see the messy version of you because sometimes the bravest thing you'll ever do, is let someone walk beside you when you're not okay.

And if all else fails, remember even duct-taped dreams can fly. You've got this.

Chapter 9

Finding Purpose in the Midst of Chaos

Success isn't some sparkling trophy waiting at the finish line. It often shows up disguised as failure, hidden in sleepless nights, doubtful stares, and hard-earned breakthroughs no one claps for. For me, success didn't arrive in a single moment. It came slowly, through scraped knees, wrong turns, small wins, and bold, sometimes reckless, leaps of faith.

Living with ADHD and dyslexia felt like running a marathon uphill in flip-flops and backward. The world wasn't built for a brain like mine. School made sure I learned that early. But the workplace is where I rewrote the rules. It's where my relentless energy, outside-the-box thinking, and hyper-focus transformed from liability to ability.

Still, I didn't land here by accident. It took grit, the raw, unfiltered kind. I had to want it more than the fear that told me to quit. And while proving the doubters wrong was satisfying, proving myself wrong was everything.

My ADHD Leap in '97

Remember when I said my wife was pregnant and money was tight? I was working full-time, clocking in at 6 a.m. and out by 2 p.m. Somewhere in the blur of exhaustion and caffeine, I made a decision that would change everything. I launched my own environmental consulting firm.

It wasn't some carefully calculated move backed by spreadsheets or a five-year plan. No, this was a full-body swan dive off a cliff, powered by stubbornness, caffeine, and the blind hope that somewhere in my backpack of chaos was a parachute, probably crumpled between a burrito receipt and a half-used field notebook.

My ADHD was the driver, the fuel, and the complete lack of caution. It whispered things like, "Hey, what if we start a business today?" and "Sleep is optional when you're chasing your dream... and also wildly overcommitted."

I'd clock out of my day job like Clark Kent in reverse, race across town, grab soil samples, run lab tests like a caffeinated raccoon with a clipboard, meet with clients, and then collapse into bed around midnight, brain still buzzing with ideas I couldn't remember by morning. Rinse. Repeat. Eat a protein bar over the sink. Repeat again.

My life back then was a balance beam made entirely of stress, adrenaline, and raw willpower, definitely not OSHA-approved. But beneath the madness, I believed in what I was building. I wasn't just hustling for money. I was clawing my way toward independence and toward a life on my terms, one where no one could tell me to sit still or stop pacing while problem-solving.

And somehow, despite zero chill and no backup plan, it worked. Within ten months, I quit my job and ran the firm full-time. The business grew. I hired staff, people who actually read instructions. I took on big projects, delivered real results, and slowly built something legit.

By the time I sold the company in 2004, it was thriving, generating real revenue, building real solutions, and giving me something I never thought I'd have as a hyperactive, scribble-prone kid from Special Ed: Pride in my own name. And, yes, maybe ADHD drove the car straight through a few fences, but it got me there.

The Gift of a Different Brain

The path wasn't paved with strategy, but it was carved with survival. Dyslexia and ADHD came with me, every day, in every report, every presentation, every email I reread a dozen times.

But slowly, I stopped seeing them as weights dragging me down and started using them as tools. Dyslexia forced me to think differently. ADHD kept me moving when others stalled.

I didn't chase roles that demanded I sit still and read all day. That would've been a slow death. Instead, I chased science. Environmental science. Geochemistry. The kind of work that lived outside the classroom. Hands-on, real-world problem-solving.

While others followed formulas, I flipped them. I made new ones. My brain was built for the unexpected. Where others saw complexity, I saw opportunity. And if it took me three times as long to write the report, fine. My work ethic was unmatched. I would finish, and it would be excellent.

Building, Burning, and Rebuilding Again

Being self-employed was a declaration. It was my way of saying, I know I don't fit the mold, so I'll build my own.

I didn't just wear a lot of hats. I made the hats, sold the hats, and probably forgot where I put the hats. CEO, field tech, janitor, lab analyst, invoice generator. I did it all. And when I couldn't do it perfectly, I hired people who could.

That was the trick, building a team that filled in my gaps. I focused on big-picture thinking and relationship-building. They focused on detail, structure, and execution. Together, we became proof that a neurodivergent guy with a vision and the right people beside him could outperform the biggest firms out there.

Clients didn't see my dyslexia. They saw the results, and they saw the hustle, the guy who showed up early, stayed late, and got the job done no matter what. That reputation was my resume, and it opened doors.

Entrepreneurship: The Good, the Bad, and the Buzzed

The lab was just the beginning. My entrepreneurial spirit couldn't sit still. I built companies the way some people buy shoes. Some worked. Some flopped. All of them taught me something.

The Analytical Laboratory thrived for seven years. I loved it until I didn't. That's the curse of ADHD: once the challenge fades, so does the interest. I started to feel the itch. So naturally, I decided to shake things up.

That's when I rebranded as an environmental consulting firm in 2001. My partner and I made a solid team, on paper. As I mentioned before, he was detail-focused but not great with people. I was all vision, all drive. We clashed. We compromised. We learned. And the business grew, until we got cocky.

Enter: a golf retail store. I know. What were we thinking?

The ADHD was thinking for me.

Let's just say, beer on tap at 9 AM is not great for business productivity. We loved golf. We didn't love retail margins. Six percent profit doesn't pay for green fees. The shop bled us dry, and eventually, we sold it. I learned that passion without profit is a hobby, and hobbies can bankrupt a company if you're not careful.

Burnout and Rebirth in Texas

Eventually, the cracks in the partnership grew too wide to ignore. I stepped away, reorganized under my own name, and moved to Austin, Texas. There, I built something I'm still proud of: a small national environmental consulting firm that made a real impact.

I learned how to scale, how to lead, and how to listen. I also learned how to build trust with clients and trust in myself. My dyslexia still tripped me up. My ADHD still pulled me in ten directions. But I kept steering the ship forward.

The key was momentum.

My mind raced constantly. I had to learn how to filter the noise. To prioritize. To delegate. To slow down long enough to build something sustainable. And it worked because, again, I refused to quit.

The Ultimate Wing-It

ADHD gave me this wild, impulsive instinct to leap before I looked, a kind of live-wire trait that made life feel like a never-ending game of "Will this work or will I regret everything?" On my best days, it was a superpower. I'd get an idea, charge into action while everyone else was still halfway through their pros-and-cons list, and nine times out of ten, I'd get there first. I could move fast, adapt faster, and throw myself into challenges without overthinking them to death. That ability to act boldly and solve problems on the fly gave me a reputation as a man who could get things done.

But there was a flip side. There always is.

My ADHD was sometimes the reason I said yes to too many things, spoke before I thought, or launched projects that had about a 30 percent chance of success, and those were the good ones. I was like a squirrel darting into traffic with a half-baked business plan and nothing but confidence to protect me. Some of those leaps led to triumph. Others where spectacular faceplants that had me questioning why anyone trusted me with adult responsibilities.

One key lesson I learned the hard way was that instinct alone isn't enough. You have to learn when to pause, when to breathe, and when to look before you leap. With some age and maturity, I learned to rein in the chaos, just enough. I didn't suppress my instincts; I just sharpened them. I made sure that my next jump had a parachute, or at least a soft landing because, while blind confidence is fun, it's a lot more fun when it actually works out.

Lessons from the Ground

Every business I built taught me lessons I couldn't have learned any other way:

- Adaptability is survival. Plans go sideways. Markets shift. People quit. You either pivot or you perish.
- Clients value reliability over polish. Show up. Follow through. Be the person they can count on when it counts.
- Partnerships require patience, clarity, and honesty. Know your strengths. Respect theirs. Communicate like it matters, because it does.
- Not every idea will work. That's not failure. It's tuition. Pay the cost, learn the lesson, and get back in the game.
- And whatever you do, don't dive into industries you know nothing about. Yes, I'm talking about the golf retail business.

My ADHD was both the engine and the risk. It gave me the energy to juggle, sprint, obsess, and execute. But it also made me prone to overextending, overpromising, and sometimes completely missing the obvious. But when I got it right, when I aimed all that energy at a problem that mattered, I could outwork, outthink, and outperform anyone in the room.

Innovation Isn't Optional

Being neurodivergent gave me one priceless gift: the ability to look at the world sideways. Where others saw rules and walls, I saw windows, loopholes, workarounds, and opportunity hiding in plain sight.

One early project still stands out. A client had a contaminated soil issue that had stumped every big-name firm they'd hired. The data was a mess, there was no clear path forward. While others got lost in analysis paralysis, I showed up, boots on the ground, hands in the dirt, and approached it differently. I didn't just solve the problem; I saved them time, money, and a massive regulatory migraine. That client stayed with me for years because I delivered.

Then came the so-called "impossible" timeline job. Every other firm passed. I said yes. ADHD on full throttle, I worked around the clock and delivered early. The client was floored. That one win kicked open doors I hadn't even knocked on yet.

Of course, not every project ended in applause. Some ideas flopped. Some went sideways. And the golf business? Yeah, that was a disaster wrapped in a kegerator and a bucket of overpriced golf balls. But every misstep gave me something I didn't have before: insight. Perspective. A thicker skin.

Now, as I look back, I know those early challenges reshaped me. Learning to let someone in, to trust, to be seen and still loved, gave me a new blueprint for how to move through the world. It wasn't just about surviving anymore; it was about living with intention. That shift, subtle as it seemed, became the foundation for lessons no classroom could teach. The most powerful truths often arrive quietly, in hard choices, in small wins, and in the people who help us rebuild.

Chapter 10

From Boardrooms to Whiteboards

Transitioning from industry to academia wasn't some grand, dramatic "drop the mic and walk off into the sunset" moment. It was more like a slow itch I couldn't scratch, a quiet, annoying little voice in the back of my mind whispering, "Hey… maybe there's more?" And like most ADHD-fueled obsessions, once it got loud enough, I couldn't unhear it.

I still remember the conversation in our kitchen the night I told my wife I wanted to leave industry for academia. She raised an eyebrow and said, "You want to trade deadlines for faculty meetings? Are you okay?" Her concern was real. She'd seen how structure kept my ADHD in check. Academia felt, to both of us, like jumping out of a plane and hoping the syllabus worked like a parachute, but she stood by me anyway, Post-it notes in hand, ready to help color-code the chaos.

After two decades of launching companies, juggling environmental crises like flaming bowling pins, and proving, both to myself and to every red-pen-wielding teacher I ever had, that ADHD and dyslexia weren't roadblocks but competitive advantages, I had an early midlife crisis of purpose. I'd built a life that looked pretty textbook successful: money, clients, cool business cards, and a ridiculous number of unread emails. But still, something in me was stirring, and for once, it wasn't just caffeine or poor life choices.

It wasn't burned out. I wasn't running from something. I was running toward something: legacy, meaning, a chance to give back to people who were still in the struggle, those who were students, dreamers, and most of all, underdogs. I wanted to help the kids sitting at the back of the class, quietly deciding they weren't smart enough. The ones who, like me, were more likely to start a small fire than get an A on a spelling test.

Part of that journey brought me back to something I'd long wanted but kept pushing aside, earning my PhD. For years, I was caught in the whirlwind of business. There was always another contract to land, another company to build, more money to chase. But in 2005, I finally drew a line in the sand and said, "Enough." I enrolled in the PhD program at Kingston University in London and went on to earn my doctorate in Environmental Sciences.

It took me six years to finish. Six years of juggling a full-time career, raising a family, being a father and husband, and grinding through one of the most mentally demanding challenges I'd ever taken on. It was difficult, stressful, and at times, downright brutal. But I did it. I wasn't new to that kind of marathon. I had already earned my master's degree while working fulltime, so I was no stranger to late nights, early mornings, and running the academic gauntlet with nothing but stubbornness and bad tasting microwaved coffee. That training hardened me for the PhD, one foot in front of the other, even when the road vanished.

It wasn't just a degree. It was my way of telling the world, and maybe more importantly, telling myself that I was good enough. Those three letters meant more than any business deal I ever had, well, maybe not when I made a killing on a business deal.

I didn't ditch industry completely. I'm still in it, knee-deep in permitting chaos, environmental consulting drama, and trying to explain to clients why, no, groundwater contamination does not magically disappear if you ignore it long enough. That work keeps me sharp. It reminds me why I fell in love with science in the first place.

Academia gave me something I couldn't find in the field or in the boardroom: a time machine. A chance to speak to the younger version of myself, the kid who felt broken and the student who thought his worth was tied to a test score or how many red marks were on his paper. It gave me the mic, and I took it to prove you can be brilliant, even if you can't spell "brilliant" on the first try.

That's why I go out of my way to spot the students who sit in the back, who avoid eye contact, who turn in half-finished because they're tired of trying and failing. I see them because I was them.

One day, after class, a student lingered. He didn't say much at first, just sort of hovered while pretending to tie his shoe three separate times. Finally, he said, "I'm not good at school. I think I'm just dumb."

It hit me like a gut punch.

I sat down next to him and said, "Let me tell you about the time I ate fried shrimp instead of going to class and got academically suspended, twice. And now I have a PhD."

He blinked. Then he laughed. And then he asked if he could come to office hours.

That's why I'm here. That's the fuel. To make sure the next kid with a firecracker brain and a fear of failure doesn't walk away before they even realize what they're capable of.

That student went on to complete his bachelor's degree in geoscience at the University of Nevada, Las Vegas. I'll never forget what he told me. "You didn't just change my path; you changed the path of my entire family."

He was a first-generation American. His parents hadn't made it past seventh grade. Now, with a university degree in hand, he was raising the trajectory of generations to come.

That student is why I'm here. That's the "why" behind every lecture, every lab, every long day. Because one person believing in you can echo through an entire family tree.

I always have to tell myself and students like me that we must resist the voices of the naysayers and choose to follow our own path to greatness, whatever that path may look like, because our potential isn't defined by their doubts but by our determination to keep moving forward.

Answering a Different Kind of Calling

When I stepped into academia, I wanted students to see that you don't have to fit neatly into the cookie-cutter mold to be successful, especially when your brain is more blender than spreadsheet. Whether it's ADHD, dyslexia, or some other internal ping-pong match, those aren't signs of failure. They're signs that you're wired for a different path. And I was living, slightly chaotic proof that different paths can lead to some pretty epic destinations.

Coming from industry, I didn't just read about environmental disasters in case studies, I was out there dealing with them, sometimes while eating gas station snacks in a truck surrounded by contaminated groundwater and three very nervous clients. I'd managed multi-million-dollar projects, navigated government red tape with a legal pad full of cryptic shorthand, and survived more meetings with engineers, attorneys, and contractors than any one person should endure.

So naturally, I thought....

"Hey, I should take all this experience into the classroom and inspire the next generation!"

Cue the plot twist I bet you saw coming. That is that industry and academia do not play well together. They're like two cousins at Thanksgiving who sit at opposite ends of the table and pretend the other one doesn't exist. Industry moves fast, breaks things, and solves problems. Academia, on the other hand, discusses the theoretical implications of possibly solving those problems someday. I walked in thinking I was bridging worlds. Most days, it felt more like I was translating between two species.

The "Busy" Paradox

One of the biggest shocks after moving into academia was discovering just how differently "busy" is defined.

In industry, forty hours is what you hit by Wednesday at 5 p.m., right after your third gas station coffee and the moment you realize you've been wearing the same steel-toed boots since Monday. A typical week? Five days of nine-to-ten-hour marathons, topped off with a generous helping of weekend "catch-up."

You don't brag about being busy in industry. You just are. Deadlines, disasters, and client drama don't care about your weekend plans, your kid's soccer game, or the fact you haven't seen a vegetable since Tuesday.

Then I entered academia. Here, "busy" sounded epic. The way some faculty described it, you'd think they were personally solving climate change, grading 14,000 lab reports, and mentoring a dozen PhD candidates while surviving solely on herbal tea and existential dread.

But then I looked around.

The day often started at 9 a.m., after coffee, light yoga, and maybe half a *New Yorker* article, and wrapped up by 3 p.m., Monday through Thursday. Fridays? Ghost town. Walk through an academic department at 2 p.m. on a Friday and you'll wonder if you missed the rapture.

Meanwhile, I'm this ADHD-fueled, hyper-tasking problem-solver surrounded by empty whiteboards, meetings about meetings, and passive-aggressive debates over who stole the good dry-erase markers. There's always one rogue marker hoarder. Always.

I was losing my mind.

In consulting, my brain was a firehose, always building, fixing, writing. In academia, it felt like being handed a Nerf gun and told, "Take it slow. Maybe do a literature review. Or just sit still and contemplate learning outcomes until your soul evaporates."

I needed action. Urgency. Impact. Not two-hour committee meetings where the highlight was: "Should we slightly adjust the mission statement… again?"

Here's the difference:

- **Industry**: "Let's solve this before lunch."
- **Academia**: "Let's schedule a meeting to discuss if it's a problem worth solving this year."

I realized I didn't need a vacation. I needed a mission. Something tangible. I needed, craved a problem with teeth and a lab full of exploding ideas. Or at the very least, a student in crisis so I could feel useful again. Open calendars and small talk just were not my love language.

Eventually, I realized I had two options. I could lose my mind, or I could fill the space with purpose. I chose purpose. I dove into real research. I rebuilt programs, and I shook up curriculum like it owed me rent. I forged partnerships with industry just to feel alive again. I craved real-world mess, the kind where work actually matters, not another six-paragraph email chain about font sizes.

The hardest part of those first two years wasn't the culture shock or the glacial pace. It was surviving Thursday afternoons without duct-taping the department into something more efficient, fueled only by whiteboard markers and caffeine-induced existential rage.

Still, I knew what I brought reality to the table. Students didn't need another textbook lecture. They needed someone who'd lived the mess, learned the hard way, and come back with stories and maybe a scar or two. I wasn't there to impress them with credentials. I was there to show them that bombing a spelling test doesn't mean you won't someday run your own firm.

More than anything, I wanted to be the voice that says, "You can," when the world keeps whispering, "You never will. Don't even think about it."

I remember the silence when I didn't know how to ask for help and the sting of being underestimated by people who didn't take the time to really see me.

I promised myself that none of my students would ever feel invisible on my watch. And yes, I let them fidget, doodle, and pace during class.

Welcome to my neurodivergent TED Talk.

The Power of Story and Struggle

Academia gave me a platform to tell the truth. I told my students that I became a scientist, so spelling wasn't a focus, just abbreviation. That I reread everything three times. That I used lists, color-coded calendars, and duct-tape-level coping strategies just to stay on track. And then I told them about the companies I built, the contracts I landed, and the projects I led to completion. That was the magic.

I was honest about my flaws because I wanted them to know that success was there for the fighters and the adapters, the ones who keep showing up even when we feel like imposters.

My students didn't need another polished academic any more than I had when I was in school. They needed a battle-worn guide who knew the terrain, someone who could say, "I've been where you are, and I made it."

Every lecture I gave, every student I mentored, became a chance to rewrite the story they'd been told about themselves. Instead of softening me, academia deepened me. It gave me space to reflect, to grow, and to keep learning while helping others do the same.

A Legacy of Possibility

I've never stopped being a consultant, and I never will. Once you've tasted the thrill of writing 200-page reports that nobody reads, it's hard to let that kind of magic go. But standing in front of a classroom, looking out at students who remind me way too much of my younger self, wide-eyed, fidgety, and possibly wondering if they left the oven on, it hits differently. It's not just about science or data or acronyms no one asked for. It's about believing that anyone no matter what their wiring, chaos, coffee dependency, or childhood trauma from spelling bees, can build something amazing.

I tell my students this, and I mean it.

"Dyslexia and ADHD are not walls. There are foundations. Use them. Don't hide from them. Adapt around your weaknesses like a ninja. That's not cheating. That's called being smarter than your frontal lobe."

Every moment I spend in academia reminds me why I traded a corner office and a company truck for dry-erase markers and students who email me at 2:47 a.m. asking if the assignment due in three hours can be turned in "late but early?" It's not just about teaching environmental science or project management. It's about transformation, and not the boring kind with spreadsheets. If even one student walks out of my class thinking, *Maybe I'm not broken. Maybe I'm just different, and that's kind of awesome*, then it's worth every sleepless night, every awkward Zoom call, and every time I trip over a backpack mid-lecture.

If I can help even one future world-changer stop apologizing for how their brain works and start owning it, that's the kind of legacy worth leaving. It's a bonus if I can finally convince someone that color-coded whiteboards are the peak of adulting.

A Scientist Among Scholars

When I first stepped into academia, it felt like I'd wandered into an intergalactic embassy where everyone spoke passive-aggressive committee-speak and progress moved at glacial speed. Coming from industry, where results, deadlines, and survival ruled, the contrast was jarring.

In consulting, you found the problem, solved it, moved on. You did it quickly with dirty hands and maybe the occasional tetanus shout. In academia, deadlines were little more than suggestions. Success meant surviving peer reviews, mastering grant-speak, and tiptoeing through email etiquette.

At first, I felt like a hummingbird in a tortoise race. I wanted to scream, "Can we solve a problem already?" But in academia, as I mentioned earlier, you don't solve problems. You discuss whether they might be problems. Eventually. After a subcommittee meeting.

Still, I adapted. That's what I do.

I was the guy who stayed late, solved problems on napkins, but academia demanded different stamina: grant rejections, approval workflows from the Dark Ages, and Zoom meetings that should've been emails months before.

My directness that was loved in industry wasn't in academia. My experience running companies and navigating regulatory chaos wasn't the usual path to tenure. Apparently, "field grit" doesn't count toward scholarly citations.

But I had been underestimated before, so, I doubled down. I showed up early, and I taught real-world lessons. I brought in client disasters, including actual mud, sometimes. And I stopped trying to squeeze into the academic box, I started reshaping it.

I wrote papers in plain English. I taught students to connect theory with reality, before reality kicked them in the shins. I shared my story: dyslexia, ADHD, imposter syndrome, the whole chaotic package. I did it because I knew some of them were carrying the same weight.

Students listen differently when you admit you once ate red-pen shame for breakfast.

Some faculty side-eyed me like I was a walking disruption (fair), but I wasn't there to conform, I was there to help my students, and somehow, between the bureaucracy and broken printers, I built something that felt real.

To anyone wondering if you belong in a place not built for your brain: you do.

And if it still doesn't feel right? Screw the blueprint. Build your own table. With cup holders. And snacks.

Of course, twenty years of real-world problem solving didn't earn instant respect. I faced questions that danced on the edge of insulting:

"Can you do research?"

"Will your mindset translate here?"

It stung. I wasn't a fresh-faced grad student. I'd earned my stripes in heat, chaos, and crisis. But now I needed to footnote my resume?

Instead of shrinking, I reframed it.

While others peer-reviewed theory, I peer-reviewed emergency response plans in hard hats. I didn't just study data, I field-tested it with steel-toes and a truck full of soil samples.

So, I leaned in. I taught students to adapt, think fast, and write reports that actually got read. I bridged theory and practice, because out there in the world, nobody's grading on a curve.

In research, I tackled real problems. I worked with colleagues who saw my "non-traditional" background as the foot in the door to impact.

Over time, things shifted. Respect didn't fall from the sky. I earned it through results, consistency, and showing up the way I always had. The same drive, just less hazard pay.

I came to understand their skepticism wasn't personal. It was systemic. Academia and industry were estranged cousins. One debates. One delivers. I was the translator. I began to see myself as the mud-covered guy asking, "What if we actually did something with this data?"

Academia needs more disruptors, more people who've done the work, who've cleaned up spills, wrangled regulators, and told terrified clients, "We've got this."

I didn't check boxes. I rewrote them.

Now I help students connect the dots, not just on paper, but in life. I teach them to think critically, to act boldly, and fail forward. I remind them that success doesn't always wear a blazer and carry a syllabus. Sometimes, it shows up in steel-toes with a coffee-stained notebook.

To anyone feeling out of place?

Good.

You're probably the one who's going to change it.

Stand out. Stay weird. Let your story speak. And if someone raises an eyebrow at your path, raise both of yours, and smile. You're not here to fit in. You're here to redefine the whole damn thing.

Translating Industry Skills to Academia

One of the greatest gifts I brought with me into academia was something no textbook could ever teach, real-world experience. You know, that unpredictable, often poorly funded adventure that starts with a client screaming, "We need this fixed yesterday," and ends with you covered in mud, clutching a clipboard, and wondering if your tetanus shot is up to date.

While I was teaching theories or formulas, I was also telling stories. From boardrooms to barren field sites. From conference calls where no one knew how to mute themselves, to crawling around contaminated sites wondering if that "mild odor" was actually deadly. I had lived science, not just studied it. I had eaten it for lunch, sometimes literally.

Pro tip: don't bring your sandwich into the lab.

The classroom became my stage, and my years in consulting were the greatest script ever written, complete with plot twists, minor explosions (only once, calm down), and more bureaucratic drama than a soap opera. I brought those stories with me, to help students see that science isn't just something you memorize for a midterm and immediately forget. It's alive. It's vital. And occasionally, it's flammable.

I could still smell the earth from the sites I visited, still hear the panic in a project manager's voice when a sample went missing, and still feel the crushing weight of deadlines that laughed in the face of sleep.

My approach paid off. My students actually listened to me. Their eyes lit up. They connected the dots. Suddenly, the dusty theory in chapter seven wasn't so dusty anymore. It had real-world impact. It mattered.

That's when I knew, I was igniting something. Curiosity. Passion. Maybe even a healthy fear of groundwater contamination.

Either way, it felt like coming full circle. From the field to the classroom, with a few detours through the chaos of life, and a whole lot of storytelling between.

As I look back, I realize how much my ADHD fueled that fire. What once felt like a curse (my racing thoughts, my constant need for stimulation, my inability to sit still), again became my secret weapon. I couldn't let go of the world outside academia. I stayed plugged in, chasing new trends, maintaining relationships with industry experts, reading, calling, connecting. That hyper-curiosity kept me sharp, and it kept me relevant.

It also gave my students an edge.

Because of those relationships, I was able to open doors many of them never thought possible. Internships, field research, real projects with real consequences, these weren't pie-in-the-sky academic exercises. These were moments when students rolled up their sleeves, got their boots muddy, and did the work. They weren't just students anymore. They were scientists, problem-solvers, and future professionals. I saw their confidence grow with each opportunity. I watched them transform.

I brought industry leaders into the classroom too, not as abstract figures on a PowerPoint slide, but as flesh-and-blood humans who shared their successes and scars. These guests were honest. They talked about failure, burnout, pivots, and perseverance. And the students soaked it in. Hearing directly from the people doing the work helped them envision their own paths. It showed them what was possible, and what would be expected.

I suppose, deep down, this work was healing something in me too. I remember my own early days, stepping into the workforce after college with a degree in hand but doubt in my heart. I was unsure, unprepared, and terrified I didn't belong. I didn't want my students to feel that way. Ever. I wanted them to enter the world not just ready, but ready to thrive.

My ADHD, once the source of so many struggles, had become my compass. It gave me relentless energy, an obsession with making connections, and an ability to see patterns and opportunities others missed. Part of my teaching became building bridges between the classroom and the job site, between theory and action, between uncertainty and confidence. My students crossed those bridges, many of them sprinting toward futures they never thought they deserved.

The world has changed. The workforce no longer waits around for someone to get up to speed. Employers want graduates who can jump in with both feet, think on the fly, and add value on day one. They don't have time for people who need months of training. They want people who can do, who can solve, who can deliver.

I understood that, because I had lived it, and I knew, especially for students with learning differences like ADHD or dyslexia, that traditional classrooms weren't always set up for their success. I saw so much potential being stifled by lectures and multiple-choice tests. These were students who thrived when they could touch, build, explore, and move. So, I redesigned my classes to meet them where they were, not by lowering standards, but by rethinking how learning happened.

I pulled from my own consulting files, real cases and real challenges. One semester, they tackled a contaminated soil site; another they mapped groundwater flow from a mining operation. These weren't sanitized problems with clean-cut answers. They were messy, complex, and alive. The students were captivated. They argued, hypothesized, tested, and debated. They learned not because they had to, but because they wanted to.

The students who were used to struggling began to shine. The ones who were always "too much," "too loud," or "too distracted" started leading teams. They brought fresh ideas to the table, made intuitive leaps others didn't see, and turned their differences into strengths. I'll never forget the look on one student's face when he realized he wasn't broken. He was brilliant. He just needed the right environment to thrive.

That's what it was all about. Creating an environment where everyone could thrive.

More than just technical knowledge, I emphasized problem-solving. I told them about my own missteps, deals that fell through, field projects that went sideways, deadlines missed. But I also shared how I adapted, how I learned, how I kept going. I wanted them to know that failure was part of the process. My students left with real skills and experience. They also left with confidence.

Theory matters, of course. It's the foundation. But without practice, it's like building a house with no roof. You need both. When my students left my program, they had both. They were ready to change the world in their own way.

I discovered my mission wasn't just to teach science; it was to transform lives. That's the legacy I'm proud of.

The Challenges of Starting Over

As much as I loved the work with students, starting over wasn't easy. Behind every written report I submitted, there were hours upon hours of rewrites. Behind every class I taught, behind every paper I published, there were drafts riddled with corrections, painstakingly combed through over and over again. My output may have looked polished, but it came at a steep price. I worked twice as hard just to keep up. From the beginning, I felt the judgment from those around me and refused to let their assumptions define me.

I leaned into what I knew best; my creativity, my drive, and my ability to connect dots others didn't even see. I wasn't going to fit neatly into the academic mold, so I started reshaping the mold itself. I pulled from my experience in the field. I designed new programs, created industry partnerships, restructured operations, and found ways to make our school more collaborative, efficient, and forward-thinking. Slowly but surely, the results began to speak for themselves. My work couldn't be ignored. By year eight, I was named Dean of the School of Science, Engineering, and Mathematics.

It was a surreal moment. Not because I didn't think I could do it, but because of how far I had come from those whispered doubts and dismissive glances. Of course, not everyone embraced the change. Some faculty clung to tradition like it was a life raft, refusing to let go of the same outdated slides they'd used for a decade. I understood the fear. Change is hard. It threatens comfort, asks questions of legacy. But I didn't come to academia to keep things the same. I came to move the needle.

My ADHD helped me do that. Where others saw chaos, I saw opportunity. Where some got stuck, I sprinted ahead. My brain never stopped firing. I juggled projects, built new programs, and found creative solutions to bureaucratic red tape. That energy was the engine behind several workforce-focused bachelor's degree programs that had never existed at my institution, designed to connect students directly with careers and industries in need of fresh, capable talent.

Leadership recognized my work and praised my vision, but that didn't mean full acceptance. My industry pace clashed with the academia. I wanted transformation in months; they preferred progress in years. I was ready to run, but sometimes it felt like I was dragging a stubborn institution behind me. Still, I kept pushing forward.

All the while, I continued publishing, building a reputation for rigorous, meaningful work in environmental science. My dyslexia, the thing so many had doubted, never went away. I still had to fight through every sentence. But my obstacles pushed me to be better, sharper, more resilient.

Hiding My Challenges

Still, even as I thrived on paper, leading departments, publishing research, and earning accolades, I was masking. Constantly.

Old habits die hard, especially the ones born from years of survival. I had learned early on how to hide the parts of myself that made others uncomfortable. And in academia, despite all our talk of inclusion and support, there was still a strong undercurrent of elitism, especially when it came to learning differences.

I heard it in passing comments about "lowering standards." I saw it in eye rolls when students asked for DRC accommodations. There were faculty who believed students requiring DRC accommodations, and by extension, people like me, simply didn't belong.

So, I kept editing. And re-editing. Every email, every memo, every grant proposal; I combed through them obsessively. My dyslexia forced me to slow down, double-check, and sometimes triple check. It was draining but necessary. Even after everything I'd achieved, I still feared the judgment that might come from a simple typo.

My ADHD was harder to mask. It pulsed through everything I did. My energy, my rapid-fire ideas, the way I jumped from thought to thought in meetings, it was obvious. Some people were overwhelmed by it. Others were inspired. But either way, it made me feel visible in a way that wasn't always comfortable.

And yet, I kept going.

My mind, always moving, allowed me to see possibilities others overlooked. My attention to patterns, my instinct for problem-solving, and my ability to hyperfocus became part of the engine driving innovation in my school. These "disabilities" became the very tools I used to excel.

I'd be lying if I said the masking didn't take a toll. There are days when I wonder how much farther I could go if I didn't have to spend so much energy appearing "neurotypical." If I could just be, without worrying how my differences might be perceived. But the world isn't always kind to those who stand out. Dropping the mask sometimes feels like standing in the middle of a room with a spotlight overhead and a sign that says: "Here are all the ways I struggle."

Still, I've come to accept that my story is not one of perfection, it's one of perseverance. And my students don't need to see perfection. They need to see what it looks like to keep going.

I've learned to embrace the power of being different. I've built programs, published research, and led institutional change because of the very things' others see as weaknesses. If my story can inspire even one student to stop hiding and start owning their journey, then all the masking, all the late nights, and all the exhaustion are worth it.

The systems that judge us need to change. And until they do, I'll keep building a path forward, not just for myself, but for every brilliant, underestimated mind still fighting to be seen.

Building Relationships with the Next Generation of Scientists

I had spent two decades in the fast-moving, often unforgiving world of industry. A world where outcomes mattered, where problems demanded immediate solutions, and where no one cared about how well you could recite a theory if you couldn't apply it. When I made the leap into academia, I saw a glaring problem: students were graduating with diplomas but without direction. They were bright, hardworking, full of potential, but often completely unprepared for the reality of the workforce.

I knew what that felt like. I'd lived it. That feeling of walking into your first job, smiling on the outside but panicking inside, wondering if you really belonged there. I didn't want that for my students. I made it my mission to do something about it.

My ADHD became my engine. My ideas came in waves, one after the next, rapid-fire, no breaks. I wasn't content with slow progress. I didn't want to wait for committees or five-year plans. I wanted partnerships. Now.

I reached out to industry leaders, company heads, and state agencies. I hit the road. I had coffee with CEOs, gave talks at conferences, toured facilities. I asked questions. I listened. And when I found an opportunity, I pounced. I didn't see students as inexperienced. I saw them as untapped talent, raw, eager, and full of promise. I just needed to connect the dots.

What might have looked like chaos from the outside, my whirlwind calendar, constant networking, relentless follow-ups, was where I thrivedBut here's something they don't tell you when you start building those bridges: not everyone wants to walk across with you. Some people, especially within your own institution, will watch your progress with suspicion.

When your colleagues see you working tirelessly, they don't always applaud. Some grow annoyed, not at the effort you put in, but at the light you seem to cast. When your programs succeed, your students shine, and your partnerships flourish, they don't always celebrate with you. Sometimes, they frown, whisper, and pull back. It doesn't matter that your work lifts students or strengthens the institution. The very act of doing, of pushing, building, thriving, can feel threating.

And when you rise, because of your hard work, your vision, your relentless drive, others may get mad at the system that's left them behind. As if your progress somehow diminished theirs. If that sounds familiar, that's because it is. It's the same thing that happened to me when I decided to go into business.

If you're going to be a bridge builder, prepare to stand alone at times. T status quo feels safe and, for many, change is scary.

But don't let it stop you.

And in the end, those bridges I built didn't just carry students forward. They carried me, past doubt, past judgment, and into a future where passion and perseverance matter more than politics or envy. That's where I found peace. And that's where I hope others find it too.

Dyslexia in the Academic World

When I entered academia, my dyslexia followed me into meetings, into emails, into every peer-reviewed article I labored over. And yet, I made a choice: I wasn't going to hide it anymore.

I began to tell my story. Honestly. I stood in front of rooms filled with students, faculty, and administrators and said, "I have dyslexia and ADHD. And I made it anyway."

It wasn't easy. Being that honest in a system that still clings to elitism can be terrifying. But I knew what was at stake. I had students who were struggling, because the system didn't know how to support them. I knew their pain. I saw myself in them. So, I spoke for them, and with them.

I became an advocate for accommodations. Not just the paperwork, but the mindset shift needed to support neurodivergent learners. I wanted faculty to understand that differences in how we learn aren't deficits, they're diversities of strength. I fought for more inclusive classrooms. I pushed for training. I demanded that we see these students, not just their struggles, but their brilliance.

And I changed the way I taught. I slowed down. I explained complex topics multiple ways. I swapped abstract theory for tangible examples. I gave students space to engage with the material in whatever way worked for them. That included visuals, field work, stories, and dialogue. I gave them the one thing I had always needed: understanding.

There were students who came to me in tears, admitting they thought they'd never make it. That they'd never feel smart. And together, we rewrote that narrative. We built strategies. We found strengths. We proved them wrong.

I spoke to my peers. I challenged their biases. I asked them to look past spelling errors and missed assignments and ask instead, "What's this student trying to tell me? What brilliance are we missing?"

Was it always well received? No. Some saw my advocacy as noise, or worse, an excuse. But I knew better. I had lived it.

Failure isn't the end, it's a chapter. A messy, vital, unavoidable chapter that teaches us how to begin again.

If there's one thing I hope I leave behind, it's proof that your challenges do not define you. How you face them does. And the courage to keep going, especially when no one else believes you can, is what makes you great.

Lessons Learned and Looking Ahead

When I look back on my journey from industry to academia, it feels like flipping through the pages of a book I once wasn't sure I had the right to write. Each chapter, full of victories, setbacks, challenges, and breakthroughs, built the person I've become. Every struggle carved out resilience I didn't know I had. Every win reminded me that I belonged, even when the world tried to convince me otherwise.

The transition wasn't easy. Academia came with its own set of rules, often unspoken, sometimes unforgiving. But each obstacle I encountered forced me to sharpen my creativity, hone my determination, and dig deeper than I ever had before. I learned to push through the doubt and stand tall when the path ahead looked impossible. And slowly, that once-impossible path became a purpose-filled road I could walk and lead others down, too.

What pushed me forward was the belief that I could make a difference, both by teaching and by transforming the very systems that once made me feel like I didn't belong. I've never stopped building bridges between academia and industry, because I know the world doesn't operate in silos. The classroom must connect to the workplace. Theory must meet practice. And students must be shown that there is more than one way to reach success.

For students who feel out of place, who have been told they're not enough, those who struggle, as I did, I've made it my mission to be their example and their advocate. I share my story openly: the battles with dyslexia, the chaos of ADHD, the constant fight to stay focused, to be taken seriously, to not get lost in systems that weren't designed for minds like mine.

I never forgot how it felt to be that struggling student sitting in the back of the room, quietly wondering if I had what it took. That memory fuels everything I do.

To anyone walking this road, don't hide who you are. Turn your secret strengths loose. Your ADHD, your dyslexia, your unique wiring; use it. Let your challenges teach you, shape you, and sharpen you for the road ahead. Your fight is what makes you unstoppable.

Never stop climbing. Never stop believing you are worthy of the goals that feel far away. Redefine success, not by someone else's standard, but by your own. Build your own box. Write your own narrative. Own your version of greatness.

The world's expectations are not rules. They're just noise. You don't have to listen.

You are enough. You always have been.

So, reach higher. Dream bigger. Fail boldly. And keep moving forward.

The stars aren't just there to be admired. They're there to be reached.

Chapter 11

The Day I Realized I Belonged

To anyone reading this who feels like you don't belong, who's been told you're not smart enough, not good enough, or not enough of whatever the world demands, I see you. I've been you. I sat where you're sitting, wondering if the struggle would ever end. Wondering if maybe, just maybe, the world was right to count me out.

I stared at pages that looked like alphabet soup. I sat in classrooms where I felt so invisible I could have committed a minor heist, and no one would have noticed. I walked down hallways with the whispers of doubt clinging to me like that one piece of toilet paper you don't realize is stuck to your shoe until it's too late.

I have heard the laughter behind my back, some of it earned, I'll admit, and I have seen the looks. You know the ones. That cocktail of pity and confusion. I have had those nights, staring at the ceiling, wondering if I was built for any of this.

Plot twist: I was…

Just not in the way they expected.

Sometimes the kid who can't pronounce "photosynthesis" without breaking into a sweat grows up to teach it, with sarcasm, swagger, and a PowerPoint that slaps.

The Day I Realized I Belonged

Life is a series of lessons, some gentle, many hard, and each one leaves a mark. They sculpt both who we are and who we're becoming.

My journey has been anything but conventional. Marked by dyslexia, ADHD, and more roadblocks than I can count, I've come to realize that true success isn't defined by what comes easily. It's born in how we respond when life gets hard. When we fall. When we're overlooked. When we question our place in the world.

While the world saw a struggling student and a scattered mind, I was quietly becoming something more. A scientist. A professor. A leader. An entrepreneur. I did this in part because of my differences.

Which brings me here, to the final chapter, the chapter I never thought I'd get to write.

What I Learned Along the Way

Success doesn't come from following someone else's map. It comes from drawing your own.

Dyslexia and ADHD refined me. They taught me to think differently, to push harder, to tackle challenges others never even saw. They also taught me that what once made me feel "less than" could become the very reason I stand out.

I'm still dyslexic. I still have ADHD. I still carry scars, emotional and psychological, from years of being misunderstood, dismissed, and underestimated. Those scars don't define my potential, but they do shape how I move through the world.

Here's something most people rarely talk about honestly. Dyslexia and ADHD do not go away. You do not outgrow them. You do not wake up one day and realize they have faded like childhood fears or old scars. They stay with you for life. They shape your days, your decisions, your relationships, and the way you move through the world. Even now, after everything I have accomplished and everything, I have overcome, they remain with me, woven into every breath I take.

As a child, I believed that one day I would finally "catch up," that my brain would eventually learn to run in the same direction and at the same speed as everyone else's. Adulthood did not fix anything. It only added more responsibility, more expectations, and more places for my mind to get tangled. My dyslexia and ADHD simply adapted, found new hiding places, and followed me into every chapter of my life.

My dyslexia shows up quietly, but its impact is sharp. It slows me down when the world expects speed. It turns simple tasks into layered puzzles. It forces me to reread, rethink, and recheck everything. The world sees the polished surface, the degrees and titles and leadership roles, but underneath all of that is still the same child who had to work twice as hard just to stand in the same place as everyone else. That effort never goes away. It only becomes more private.

ADHD is louder. It does not sit politely in the background. It surges through me like electricity. It speeds me up when I need calm and locks me in when I need to let go. It makes me intense, driven, focused, impatient, and overwhelmed, sometimes within the same hour. I have spent a lifetime trying to contain a mind that does not want to be contained. It feels like trying to hold a tornado inside a glass jar. You might keep it steady for a moment, but eventually it rattles loose, and everything starts spinning.

In the workplace, that spinning was always there. I could feel it in meetings, deadlines, critiques, and conversations that required me to balance clarity, patience, and speed. I hated being misunderstood and hearing people assume I was too blunt, too direct, too fast, or too intense. They did not see the battle happening beneath the surface. They did not feel the rush of thoughts climbing over each other inside my mind, all of them demanding attention at once. There were days I came home exhausted, questioning my worth and wondering if my brain simply was not made for the world, I was trying so hard to succeed in.

Sometimes, I think that feeling is what eventually led me to step out and build something of my own. When you work for yourself, you can build a world that matches your wiring. You can create systems that make sense to your mind instead of forcing yourself into systems that never fit. When the day overwhelmed me, I shared those moments with my wife. I came home raw and frustrated and often felt as if I were fighting a current, I could not swim against. She grounded me. She reminded me that I was not broken. She helped me breathe again. Without her, I am not sure I would have survived some of the storms in my own head.

The hardest truth, the one that still hurts the most, is how much ADHD affects the people I care about even today. No matter how old I am or how self-aware I try to be, ADHD never stops swirling in my mind like a storm that refuses to calm. It is a tornado made of thoughts, emotions, impulses, fears, and exhaustion. It spins without warning. It consumes everything around it. Unless someone has lived with ADHD themselves, they cannot understand how relentless it is.

People may know about ADHD, but they do not feel what I feel. They do not feel the racing mind, the interruptions I never intended, the intensity that does not match the moment, the overwhelm that strikes out of nowhere, the distraction that feels like betrayal, or the guilt that floods me after every misunderstanding.

My relationships have suffered because of it. Not once or twice, but throughout my entire life. I have watched connections crack under the weight of misunderstandings I did not have the power to prevent. People have walked away because they thought I did not care, when the truth was that I cared too much and could not slow the storm inside me long enough to show it. Each time it left a mark, a quiet ache, and a sense of being difficult without ever trying to be.

I have lost opportunities, friendships, and important connections because of my ADHD and dyslexia. Doors closed that I never meant to close. Relationships slipped away, not because I did not value them, but because I could not keep up with the expectations or emotional rhythms that others needed. I have missed chances to grow, to belong, and to be understood. Some moments still sting when I think about them, things I said too quickly, things I forgot too easily, things I felt too intensely. None of it was intentional. None of it was a lack of care. The storm in my mind pushed people away even when all I wanted was to bring them closer.

Even now, I am aware of how ADHD shapes my reactions, my communication, my emotional responses, and the way I show up for people. Awareness does not stop the storm. It only lets me see the damage more clearly.

I wish people understood how exhausting it is to fight a brain that never rests. I wish they understood how much effort it takes to stay steady, to stay present, and to stay gentle. I wish they knew I am trying, always trying. And I wish they could see the love that sits beneath the chaos.

My dyslexia and ADHD shaped not only the challenges in my life, but also the strength it took to build something meaningful anyway. I did not succeed because I escaped these conditions. I succeeded because I carried them. The weight of that has carved both my resilience and my scars.

Why I Was Successful— Why You Can Be Too

These are the choices I made every day.

- I never gave up, even when quitting felt easier.
- I stopped trying to "fix" myself and started embracing who I was.
- I built systems to support my brain: calendars, color codes, checklists, some held together with metaphorical (and sometimes literal) duct tape.
- I leaned into my strengths: creativity, energy, intuition, and out-of-the-box thinking.
- I surrounded myself with people who believed in me when I forgot how to believe in myself.
- Most of all, I stopped apologizing for how my brain works.

For Those Walking a Similar Path

To anyone navigating life with dyslexia, ADHD, trauma, or any form of neurodivergence: You are not broken. You're becoming. Your challenges aren't flaws. They're your edge. They give you superpowers most people can't begin to understand.

I know it doesn't always feel like power. Some days, it just feels like survival. Some days, you'll want to disappear. I've been there. But something always whispered to me:

"If I stay small, I'll never become who I'm meant to be."

Neither will you.

Here's what I've learned:
- Perseverance Pays Off: I've been knocked down by other people's expectations, my own inner doubts, and systems that were never designed for someone like me. But I got up. That's what made the difference.
- Your Perspective is Your Strength: The way I connect dots, solve problems, and innovate comes directly from how my brain is wired. What some saw as a deficit became my greatest advantage.
- Community Matters: Behind every moment I almost quit was someone who pulled me through, my wife, my mentors, my students. Find your people. Hold them close.
- Failure is a Teacher: Every fall taught me more than any win ever could. Failure isn't the opposite of success. It's the path to it.
- Stay Curious: Let your hunger to grow override your fear of falling. Ask questions. Challenge assumptions. Stay weird.
- Reject Limiting Beliefs: Other people's doubts are not your ceiling.

And When You Get There…

Because you will get there, wherever "there" is for you, look around. And then turn around.

Reach out your hand and pull someone else up. Be the person you once needed. The one who says, *"You belong here. You always did."*

The world wasn't built for minds like ours, which is exactly why we're here: to rebuild it.

So, if you remember nothing else, remember this:

You don't need to be perfect.

You just need to keep going, one imperfect, relentless step at a time.

Finally, "I didn't succeed because I escaped my challenges—I succeeded because I carried them."

Letter to the Reader

Dear Reader,

If you made it to this page, thank you for walking beside me through the fire, the fog, and the fried shrimp moments. For sitting with the awkward pauses, the painful flashbacks, the self-doubt, and the moments of quiet defiance. If my story stirred something in you, whether it was anger, laughter, or a sense of finally feeling seen, then this book did its job.

I wrote it because I spent too much of my life feeling like I didn't belong. And if I could go back and whisper anything to that younger version of me, or to the version of you that still questions their worth, it would be, "You are not broken. You are a custom build."

Yes, the world can be loud, cold, and unkind to minds that work differently. But that difference is your strength.

This book isn't the end of my story; it's the beginning of a new conversation. One where neurodivergence isn't hidden, masked, or "managed," but celebrated. One where schools, workplaces, and families stop asking, "What's wrong with you?" and start asking, "What do you need to thrive?"

Take the parts of this book that resonate. Share them. Pass this book to someone who is in the trenches right now, someone fighting invisible battles and wondering if they'll ever feel smart enough, capable enough, enough.

Tell them they're not alone either.

Always rooting for you,

Douglas B. Sims, PhD
The Dyslexic Scientist

Bibliography

American Psychiatric Association. (2013). Diagnostic and statistical manual of mental disorders (5th ed.). Arlington, VA: American Psychiatric Publishing.

Barkley, R. A. (2020). Taking charge of ADHD: The complete, authoritative guide for parents (4th ed.). Guilford Press.

Biederman, J., & Faraone, S. V. (2005). Attention-deficit hyperactivity disorder. The Lancet, 366(9481), 237-248.

Branson, R. (2017). Finding my virginity: The new autobiography. Portfolio.

Corcoran, B., & Christy, B. (2003). Use what you've got, and other business lessons I learned from my mom. Penguin.

Eide, B. L., & Eide, F. F. (2011). The dyslexic advantage: Unlocking the hidden potential of the dyslexic brain. Plume.

Faraone, S. V., Biederman, J., & Mick, E. (2015). The age-dependent decline of attention deficit hyperactivity disorder: A meta-analysis of follow-up studies. Psychological Medicine, 36(2), 159–165. https://doi.org/10.1017/S003329170500471X

Faraone, S. V., Sergeant, J., Gillberg, C., & Biederman, J. (2015). The worldwide prevalence of ADHD: Is it an American condition? World Psychiatry, 2(2), 104-113.

Fletcher, J. M., Lyon, G. R., Fuchs, L. S., & Barnes, M. A. (2007). Learning disabilities: From identification to intervention. Guilford Press.

Fuchs, D., & Fuchs, L. S. (2006). Introduction to response to intervention: What, why, and how valid is it? Reading Research Quarterly, 41(1), 93-99.

Hammond, C. (2012, September 12). How Steven Spielberg's dyslexia diagnosis made sense of his struggles. ABC News. https://abcnews.go.com/Health/steven-spielbergs-dyslexia-diagnosis-made-sense-struggles/story?id=17214886

Hallowell, E. M., & Ratey, J. J. (2011). Driven to distraction: Recognizing and coping with attention deficit disorder. Anchor Books.

Hinshaw, S. P., & Scheffler, R. M. (2014). The ADHD explosion: Myths, medication, money, and today's push for performance. Oxford University Press.

Lyon, G. R., Shaywitz, S. E., & Shaywitz, B. A. (2003). A definition of dyslexia. Annals of Dyslexia, 53(1), 1-14.

Madaus, J. W., & Shaw, S. F. (2006). Disability services in postsecondary education: Impact of IDEA and Section 504. Journal of Developmental Education, 30(1), 12-21.

Newman, L. A., Wagner, M., Knokey, A. M., Marder, C., Nagle, K., Shaver, D., & Wei, X. (2011). The post-high school outcomes of young adults with disabilities up to 8 years after high school: A report from the National Longitudinal Transition Study-2 (NLTS2). National Center for Special Education Research.

Nigg, J. T. (2017). Getting ahead of ADHD: What next-generation science says about treatments that work—and how you can make them work for your child. Guilford Press.

Pelham, W. E., Fabiano, G. A., & Massetti, G. M. (2005). Evidence-based assessment of attention-deficit hyperactivity disorder in children and adolescents. Journal of Clinical Child and Adolescent Psychology, 34(3), 449-476.

Pennington, B. F. (2009). Diagnosing learning disorders: A neuropsychological framework (2nd ed.). Guilford Press.

Pliszka, S. R. (2007). Pharmacologic treatment of attention-deficit/hyperactivity disorder: Efficacy, safety, and mechanisms of action. Neuropsychology Review, 17(1), 61-72.

Quinn, P. O., & Madhoo, M. (2014). A review of attention-deficit/hyperactivity disorder in women and girls: Uncovering this hidden diagnosis. The Primary Care Companion for CNS Disorders, 16(3), 13r01596.

Scarborough, H. S. (1990). Very early language deficits in dyslexic children. Child Development, 61(6), 1728-1743.

Shaywitz, S. E. (2003). Overcoming dyslexia: A new and complete science-based program for reading problems at any level. Knopf.

Snowling, M. J., & Hulme, C. (2021). The science of reading: A handbook. Wiley-Blackwell.

Stanovich, K. E. (1988). Explaining the differences between the dyslexic and the garden-variety poor reader: The phonological-core variable-difference model. Journal of Learning Disabilities, 21(10), 590-604.

Torgesen, J. K. (2002). The prevention of reading difficulties. Journal of School Psychology, 40(1), 7-26.

Vellutino, F. R., Fletcher, J. M., Snowling, M. J., & Scanlon, D. M. (2004). Specific reading disability (dyslexia): What have we learned in the past four decades? Journal of Child Psychology and Psychiatry, 45(1), 2-40.

Wilens, T. E., & Spencer, T. J. (2010). Understanding attention-deficit/hyperactivity disorder from childhood to adulthood. Postgraduate Medicine, 122(5), 97-109.

Willcutt, E. G. (2012). The prevalence of DSM-IV attention-deficit/hyperactivity disorder: A meta-analytic review. Neurotherapeutics, 9(3), 490-499.

Wolf, M., & Bowers, P. G. (1999). The double-deficit hypothesis for the developmental dyslexias. Journal of Educational Psychology, 91(3), 415-438.

Appendices

Resources for Dyslexia

Dyslexia is not a barrier to success, it's a challenge that, when understood and embraced, can lead to incredible growth and achievement. Here are some valuable resources to help individuals with dyslexia and those supporting them:

<u>Books</u>
- "Overcoming Dyslexia" by Dr. Sally Shaywitz
A scientifically backed exploration of dyslexia, including diagnosis, intervention strategies, and the positive outcomes for individuals with dyslexia when they receive the right support.
- The Dyslexic Advantage:Unlocking the Hidden Potential of the Dyslexic Brain by Eide and Eide
- "The Gift of Dyslexia" by Ronald D. Davis
This book discusses dyslexia as a gift rather than a disability, providing a powerful approach to help people with dyslexia tap into their unique learning strengths.
- Add in here Taking Charge of Adult ADHD by Russell Barkley (#1 book)
- "ADHD: A Hunter in a Farmer's World" by Thom Hartmann
A fresh look at ADHD from the perspective of evolutionary psychology, offering a deep dive into the strengths of ADHD traits and how to channel them into success.
- "Driven to Distraction" by Dr. Edward M. Hallowell and Dr. John J. Ratey
A thorough guide on ADHD, discussing its symptoms, how it affects everyday life, and actionable advice for managing ADHD effectively, both personally and professionally.
- "The ADHD Advantage: What You Thought Was a Diagnosis May Be Your Greatest Strength" by Dale Archer
This book reframes ADHD from a deficit-based disorder to

a strength-based perspective, showcasing how people with ADHD can leverage their traits to achieve success.

Websites

- **International Dyslexia Association (IDA)**
  Offers extensive research, resources, and advocacy support, helping individuals understand dyslexia, navigate education systems, and access accommodations.
- **Understood.org**
  Provides tools, articles, and expert advice for parents and educators to manage dyslexia, ADHD, and other learning challenges, empowering individuals to succeed academically and socially.
- **Dyslexia Advantage**
  Focuses on highlighting the unique strengths of individuals with dyslexia, offering insights into how these traits can translate into success in both academic and professional settings.
- **ADDitude**
  A comprehensive online resource for individuals with ADHD, offering expert articles, tools, and tips on managing symptoms, improving focus, and navigating life with ADHD.
- **Learning Ally**
  Provides audiobooks and learning resources for individuals with learning disabilities, making education more accessible and helping students with dyslexia reach their full potential.
- **The National Center for Learning Disabilities (NCLD)**
  A non-profit that advocates for individuals with learning disabilities, offering resources on legal rights, educational policies, and practical solutions for overcoming learning challenges.

Organizations

Child Mind Institute
Yale Center for Dyslexia
- Dyslexia Foundation
  Supports research, education, and advocacy for dyslexic individuals, working to improve awareness and access to interventions for those affected by dyslexia.
- Learning Disabilities Association of America (LDA)
  A major organization providing resources for individuals with learning disabilities, including advocacy, legal support, and information on how to manage learning challenges effectively.
- National Attention Deficit Disorder Association (ADDA)
  Provides resources and a community for individuals with ADHD, focusing on promoting awareness, providing support, and creating strategies for living successfully with ADHD.
- The International ADHD Coach Academy (IACTA)
  Focuses on training professional coaches who work with individuals with ADHD, providing them with the skills needed to help clients achieve personal and professional success.
- CHADD (Children and Adults with Attention-Deficit/Hyperactivity Disorder)
  A national organization that provides advocacy, resources, and a network of support for individuals affected by ADHD, with programs to assist with both diagnosis and management.

About the Author

Douglas B. Sims, PhD, is a distinguished environmental soil scientist, entrepreneur, and academic leader whose career spans over three decades. Dr. Sims has achieved remarkable success, founding and building four thriving environmental consulting companies that operated on a national scale before strategically selling them. Alongside his entrepreneurial accomplishments, he pursued his academic goals with determination, earning a BA, MS, and PhD while navigating the challenges of dyslexia and ADHD. His academic journey has culminated in publishing high-impact research in peer-reviewed journals and authoring books that contribute to the broader scientific and professional communities.

In 2011, he transitioned from industry to academia, bringing with him a wealth of experience and a proven track record of innovation and leadership. Over the past 15 years, he has made a significant impact in higher education, starting as an environmental science instructor and rising to become the Dean of the School of Science, Engineering, and Mathematics at a leading community college. Under his leadership, the school has flourished, with a strong focus on student success, workforce development, and cutting-edge interdisciplinary programs that connect education with real-world applications.

Dr. Sims's career reflects a unique blend of scientific expertise, entrepreneurial spirit, and a passion for leadership. His dedication to advancing environmental science, fostering innovation, and nurturing the next generation of professionals stands as a testament to his ability to bridge the worlds of industry and academia. Married to his college sweetheart since the early 1990s, Dr. Sims and his wife are proud parents of two grown children, further underscoring his commitment to balancing professional success with personal fulfillment.